DISCOVERING YOUR PRAYER DNA:
PRAYING WITH PASSION, PURPOSE, AND POWER

Bishop Darryl F. Husband SR. D.Min.

DISCOVERING YOUR PRAYER DNA:
PRAYING WITH PASSION, PURPOSE, AND POWER

©2013 Life More Abundant Ministries

Published by LuLu.com

Printed in the United States of America
All rights reserved. No part of this publication may be reproduced, stored in a retrieval system or transmitted in any form or by any means- electronic, mechanical, photocopy, recording or any other- without the prior written permission of the publisher. The only exception is brief quotations in printed reviews.

Unless otherwise noted; Holy Bible, New International Version®. Copyright © 1973, 1978, 1984 International Bible Society. Used by permission of Zondervan. All rights reserved.

Scripture taken from the Amplified® Bible,
Copyright © 1954, 1958, 1962, 1964, 1965, 1987 by The Lockman Foundation Used by permission." (www.Lockman.org)

Scripture quotations identified as KJV are from the King James Version of the Bible.

Scripture taken from The Message. Copyright ©1993, 1994, 1995, 1996, 2000, 2001, 2002. Used by permission of NavPress Publishing Group."

Scripture taken from the New American Standard Bible®, Copyright © 1960,1962,1963,1968,1971,1972,1973,1975,1977,1995 by The Lockman Foundation. Used by permission." (www.Lockman.org)

ISBN: 978-1-304-15521-4

Dedication

This book like every book I have written is dedicated first to The Lord Jesus who radically transformed my life. The door to my heart never closes for him. That intimacy was the key to the image in which He created me to walk.

To my beautiful bride who allows me freedom to pursue God continuously and to dictate what he says, so others can be empowered.

To my children whom I love dearly and cannot imagine what my life would have been without them. To my youngest two, Darryl and Gabriella, who without a doubt helped add years to my life by coming when I should've been rearing grand babies. You are my pride, joy and angel. To Daytriel, my big Baby Girl, who now has a family of her own, may you model integrity and worship to them. To Eric, my oldest, whom I am well pleased; as I see you continue to grow in God and ministry. And to Jason, whom my prayer daily, is that God would make a way for you to truly know the heart of your father for yourself and meet your siblings. We love you.

To the Life More Abundant Ministries family (Mount Olivet and LI.F.E. Church), for pushing me into my divine destiny.

To My sons and daughters in the A.M.E.N fellowship; you all are an inspiration to me.

Finally, this book is dedicated to the many prayer warriors in the army of intercessors around the world, beginning with Bishop W. Wellington Boone and Bishop William Murphy Jr. I say thanks to you for seeing in me something worthy of leading others into the trenches to fight for the Kingdom. It's an honor to serve you both.

Acknowledgements

To my Administrator and Vice President of Life More Abundant Publishing, Elder Sandra Johnson: Thanks for your tireless service to the kingdom, to our ministry and to your spiritual father. Your dedication to detail helps make me a better leader.

Thanks Elder Hugh, you are a true servant. You never cease to capture the essence of what Jesus looks like. You continue to inspire me with your passion. I am honored to be called a father in your eyes. You have covered all of my work artistically and in prayer.

Thanks to Joy for your desire to continue to serve. May your health increase immediately so you can return to service.

Thanks to Bishop Bridgett Johnson, Elder Tara Culton and Jasmine Baker: for helping to make certain we met our deadline.

Thanks to Minister Larry Cozart for your creativity with our book covers, and to team LMAM for all your dedicated service.

Table of Contents

Dedication 5
Acknowledgements 7
Chapter 1 "An Upside Down House" 11
Chapter 2 One Band, One Sound 20
Chapter 3 Taking Your City: Spiritual Mapping 30
Chapter 4 Entrance Exam 42
Chapter 5 The Worship Intercessor 46
Chapter 6 The Prophetic Intercessor 59
Chapter 7 The Research Intercessor 76
Chapter 8 The Warfare Intercessor 88
Chapter 9 The Bridal Intercessor 108
Chapter 10 The Family Intercessor 122
Chapter 11 The Soul/Salvation Intercessor 139
Chapter 12 Mercy and Grace Intercessor 160
Chapter 13 The Crisis Intercessor 175
Chapter 14 The Governmental Intercessor 194
Chapter 15 The General Intercessor 212
Chapter 16 The Financial Intercessor 225
Bibliography 256
About The Author 261
Other Books by Bishop Darryl F. Husband, Sr. 263

Chapter 1 "An Upside Down House" Turning The House Right Side Up

There is a famous story told about Charles Spurgeon, and the great throngs of people he preached to at London England's Metropolitan Tabernacle. It is said that people would come from the world over to hear him and ask the same question time and time again, " Dr. Spurgeon, to what do you attribute your great success?" He would lead some of the people on a short tour. Shortly after beginning the tour he would begin asking them to accompany him to the "boiler room". You can imagine the response of the guests. They were thinking just as you are now, "Why would anyone want to see the boiler room?" Of course, after the continual mentioning of the boiler room to the tourists, they would agree, if for no other reason, to accommodate the guide so they could continue to see the more interesting sites. Then, he would open the door to the boiler room, where 700 people would be bowed in prayer and praising God for the worship service soon to begin. Spurgeon did not attribute his success to education, elegance of speech, nor excellence of administration. He contributed it to the power of intercession as its foundation.

Italian philosopher Niccolò Machiavelli makes a noteworthy point that I believe needs to be heard, because many ministries in the body of Christ are built today with malignant materials. He said, "He who has not first laid his foundation, may be able with great ability to lay them afterwards, but they will be laid with trouble to the architect and danger to the building."[1] Building a strong foundation for any structure is the most critical thing that will determine its durability and longevity. Every wise builder of any home, business, ministry or personal life, knows this. The wisest of all builders left these words with his listeners after preaching/teaching on a multitude of areas which he considered foundational for life lived in the kingdom of God. He said,

> "24 "Therefore everyone who hears these words of Mine and acts on them, may be compared to a wise man who built his house on the rock. 25 And the rain fell, and the floods came, and the winds blew and slammed against that house; and *yet* it did not fall, for it had been founded on the rock. 26 Everyone who hears these words of Mine and does not act on them, will be like a foolish man who built his house on the sand. 27 The rain fell, and the floods came, and the winds blew and slammed against that house; and it fell—and great was its fall." Matthew 7: 24 – 27 (NASB)

That said, you would think any contractors would be insane who upon showing you the designs of your house and explaining how they planned to build it, said to you, "Okay we are going to build the roof first. Then sir, we will build the side panels, a nice floor, first-class hardwood in some areas and tile in the others. We have of course saved the best for last. We will put a nice finishing touch on the house by building you a beautiful foundation." Now, if the truth be told, that is exactly how a house "should" be built, exactly with that order in mind as the builder builds. It sounds crazy I know. Let me explain that before you determine that I should be committed to a hospital for brain damage. The foundation must be strong

---

[1] Niccolo Machiavelli, *The Prince* (Boston: Bedford/St. Martin's, 2005),

enough to support everything that sets on it. Therefore, everything should be at least fully considered, before the foundation is built. If the expectation of the building has great weight, then the foundation must be deep and strong. Therefore we must know the rest of the building before we exact the foundation. Ok? Now you believe I am a genius, don't you?

Seasons Change, One Thing Doesn't

We have gone through what appears to be seasons in the church, where one of the various "gifting" in the body of Christ have risen to be more dominant than the other. While the local pastor seems to be a constant, we have seen over the last 30 years, the season of the "televangelists." The "Billy Graham" type of evangelists who drew thousands to tents and stadiums to get saved had a tremendous impact on the growth of the church. Beyond that 30 years, Smith Wigglesworth, Amy McPherson, A. A. Allen, Kathryn Kuhlman and Jack Coe. Then came Oral Roberts. They impacted the church in the area of faith healing and began an era of "Word of Faith", and the "teachers" movement. Over the past 20 years this teacher's movement has changed church as we know it everywhere. We seemed to move then to the era/season of the prophetic and apostolic at the same time. Some say it is the last age before the coming of Jesus. I know not the day nor hour for his arrival, but one thing I do know and that is, I want us all to be ready. In ALL of these eras, there is ONE thing that undergirded every move of God we have experienced. That ONE thing, is the foundational structure that must never be overlooked and always must be improved upon in the lives of the believers. That ONE thing, is none other than prayer.

Turn The Light On

Jesus told the disciples that they were (as we are) "the light of the world". The "church" is the light of the world. Without us, the world sits in utter darkness. It has not the ability to see its way to the purpose for which it was created. When we are therefore distracted vessels of light, which means our light is compromised or obscured by worldly things; those whom were called to lead are in danger. When our light has been dimmed, it causes stumbling on a path that we were meant to make clear. We are God's amazingly graced lighthouses on the dark waters of life. The light in us is the Word of God, but the switch that keeps the light shining or provides the power for its illumination, is prayer.

The Cultural Switch

When I was a kid, we used to ride with our parents or grandparents and play a game called "that's mine". We would see a car we liked or a boat we liked or even a house we liked and the first to see it would yell out, "that's my house" or "that's my boat" etc. if my brother or sister claimed something bigger or looked better or prettier than I had, I would look for something to trump theirs. Envy was actually at the core of the game. The church today has some of these tendencies. (Stay with me; I am going where the *true* intercessors need to "tarry."

"My house shall be called a house of prayer for all nations," (Mark 11:17b) is a call to intercession. While I see a tremendous move of God in the area of an intercession in the young European American culture, I do not see it as it once was (priority number one) in the African-American culture. In some sense the house has been turned upside down in these two cultures. It's as if they have played the "that's mine" game. What I am referring to is this. African-Americans, which having been labeled as "the underclass", always felt that it was in their best interest to believe God through prayer, even when it was "illegal" to be able to read. It was prayer, and the intercession that was made on behalf of the dominant culture that was credited as the single most effective tool for survival and success. The more survival and success surfaced, it brought with it more integration into the "normal" flow of society. Acceptance and success seemed to squeeze out the means to the end. The means was prayer. The end was freedom/deliverance from bondage. Now, even though church is still a large part of community, it has become an event to be a part of and not so much an "experiencing of God" that changes us, so we can change the world. Arts and the charisma of the preacher/five-fold ministry gift have often replaced sound doctrine and prayer. Time clocks have interfered with "Tarrying."

While the African-American church has tried to push for membership growth and mega-church modeling to validate all worth, there is a move in the Euro culture towards 24 hour houses of prayer and total submission to the will of God. Talking about inversion! The house has turned upside down! The privileged class seeks the "deliverance God", who has always been known as *the* source of strength enabling people to endure anything and survive. And the so-called "underclass" seeks the "gods" that lived in the people who were called oppressive, with whom they had serious issues. Now here is the KINGDOM question. What would happen if ALL of us, who claimed we knew Him, got on the same page? You see, what made the so-called "underclass" know that they could not really be labeled, was prayer. Even with less money and little education, the people knew that they belonged to the Kingdom of God and that meant they were royalty even if they looked and were treated like rags. This is The Generation, where all of us should come together.

The Generation Of The Kingdom Class

The kingdom class has no agenda but the one God gives them. They are not labeled by positions, or jobs, or economic stability, land acquisitions or investments. They are called such, because of their submission to the clarion call to change the world and are clear that it begins from the bottom up, not the top down. The knee is the place of promotion. Prostrate is the proper position for vision. And without vision, "a redemptive revelation" of God, death is the end result. We are not talking mere physical death, but social, psychological, and spiritual. The meaning of life itself and all its intended joy (as opposed to worldly pleasures), has its foundation in our ability to see clearly. Seeing out of "eternal" spectacles or having an understanding of eternity while you are here, is what it's all about. That alone will change you. However, to see out of heaven's glasses in the earth, we have to be in constant contact with the Father.

The challenge of this kingdom class is to put together a strategy to meet the continual attacks of the enemy, on our culture. That strategy must have covenant and Christ Kingdom conformity at its core. Have you ever thought about what could happen if we all decided to discover our spiritual gifts and partner with people in our particular gift area so we could compound our effort and effect on the enemy? What if we did the same thing in the area of intercession? I mean, what if we found out each of our special areas of intercession and teamed up with people of like passion, to pray? What If The House Of God Really Did Become The House Of Prayer? Why not find out what every one of us is passionate about and train up an army of intercessors. Special Forces, teams of soldiers, focused on specific assignments? Is that now what the body is supposed to do? Order makes a difference.

General Practitioners: The Family Physician

In the British Journal of General Practice, November 1995, there started to be a decline in the morale in the area of physicians going into GP or general practice. In my childhood, it was common practice for physicians, but Health Day news, our Internet service that provides daily health news for consumers and medical professionals, reported in December of 2012, that fewer medical students are choosing careers in primary care and are opting to become specialists instead. Again, be patient, I promise you I am going somewhere with this!

Years ago (as in decades), we stopped using one teacher to teach all the subjects to every grade level. We recognized the need for specialist to concentrate on one area and become experts of that area. This was done so they could give students the best training from people totally focused in an area, thereby getting the greatest possible results from the students. Then, the next generation of students and teachers would be even more skilled, creating a more advanced society. (Hold your horses, I think you see where I'm going though).

In the area of the law, there are people who specialize in the area of defense, prosecution, criminal, antitrust, case law, civic, class action, bankruptcy, constitutional, health care, labor, marital, tax, real estate... And while some could help you in common law, when you need tax help, they may refer you to a colleague better suited to serve your special needs, so that you could get the absolute best out of your situation.

The armed services have specialists. They go through extensive training in order to make sure that they are well equipped to serve their very important post. They understand that their lack of preparation, or absence of attention in an assignment could cost lives and possibly a breach, that could set back the advances of their country. (Okay, I won't make you wait any longer)

Special Forces

You are Special Forces! You are getting ready for intensive training. This book is your basic training guide to help you understand your place. For years, the church has operated its ministries and also many of its schools as "general practitioner training centers". While there will always be a need for general practitioners, there is also a great need for specialist work, trained specifically for one area of expertise, so that this particular area is foundationally strong. We have all heard the term "Jack of all trades, master of none." Well, our goal is to build an army of master prayer warriors, so that the foundational structure of the church in every city, is secure and able to handle every attack. They should be strong towers, seeing the enemy coming from afar, hearing its battle strategies in advance and able to fortify the city, so that the enemy cannot penetrate it. The church is there as a wall of prayer so that the needs of the communities are met. Notice that I said, "THE CHURCH singular. We are one body in several locations.

Symphony Of Sound

Heretofore, we have been praying, but it has sounded like the orchestra warming up before the concert. Each instrument making noise, and we know they are present, but the conductor has not called them to order. When order comes, all of the like instruments, and those who play them, are seen gathering in their particular sections. Once there, they watch for the conductor and eagerly await their turn to play. They now become a part of something magnificent. The sound is in sync. Each piece piercing the atmosphere in perfect timing as they present the perfect satisfaction in the heart of the listener, drowning out every distraction of past or future issues.

Prayer, in its right timing, per se, calms the heart of man, excites the heart of God, and attacks the distracter of "life more abundant." It's time for us to get to our places in the orchestra. We are getting ready to create a sound that will make the enemy crazy! From every direction, unhindered, unified intercession. Let's see what's next? Are you ready?

Chapter 2 One Band, One Sound

Several years back, 2002 to be exact, there was a movie out entitled "Drum Line." The young star of the film, Nick Cannon, played a very talented drummer, Devon Miles, who was trying to gain acceptance by always showing off his skills. There were times that he didn't care about embarrassing others or following leadership. As a result, he became costly to his fellow band members. He often thought of himself as a one-man show. After several hard lessons that addressed his pride issues, the band director, Dr. Lee (played by Orlando Jones), kicked him off the team. It was through expelling him, and a few other setbacks, that these messages were finally able to get through to Devon: 1) "You have to learn to follow before you can lead"; and 2) "One band, One sound".[2] These were two of the confrontations that were a part of Devon's "school of humility", and must be a part of ours as well, if we are to make the kind of impact we should in the world.

One band, one sound, is really what we are after in the church. Finding our place in the body allows the church to function at the highest level of influence in the world. Just as the church is at its best when we know our special gifts, it is further fortified when it understands its "prayer personality", or discovers it's "Prayer DNA".

---

[2] http://www.imdb.com/title/tt0303933/Accessed June 12, 2013

Kings and Priests

Before we delve into our prayer DNA or personality however, it is important to understand who we are and what we carry. Our Prayer DNA is actually a specific area of passion we have in the area of prayer and is a byproduct of who we are spiritually.

John Maxwell has been quoted many times saying, "Everything rises and falls on leadership." I am convinced that this is true not only in your home, with your family, or on your job with the manager/boss/CEO etc. It is also true with the world. The church (that would be us), is called to bring leadership to the world. The power to lead comes from the Word of God and is fueled by prayer.

Derek Prince, theologian, author and spiritual father/mentor to many, wrote, "God has vested in us his - believing people on earth - authority by which we may determine the destinies of nations and governments. He expects us to use our authority both for his glory and for our own good." [3] When God gave to us eternal life, which includes "life more abundantly" here, it came with expectations that we would use what he put in us as a weapon against the kingdom of darkness, to fight for the freedom of entangled souls. Knowing who we are and what is in us is critical to their freedom. We are kings and priests! Prince notes, "Here we play our part in the double ministry of Christ. As kings, we rule with him, as priests, we share his Ministry of prayer and intercession. We must never seek to separate these two functions from each other. If we would rule as kings, we must serve as priests. The practice of our priestly ministry is the key to the exercise of our kingly authority. It is through prayer and intercession that we administer the authority that is ours in the name of Jesus." [4]

---

[3] Derek Prince, *Shaping History through Prayer and Fasting* (New Kensington, PA: Whitaker House, 2002), 33

Not Just A Church That Prays… A Praying Church

If indeed it was the passion of Jesus to never go a day without communicating with the father, and as a result, he lived dominating his way back to heaven, why are we clueless? Aren't the breadcrumbs that lead to the "big house" large enough? I would rather not repeat myself, but didn't he say "my house" will be called a house of prayer? There are several clues there, which should make us clear on what we are to be about as the church and as persons:

1. The possessive pronoun "my" suggests that we have no say so in setting the fundamental rules of the house. It's not ours, it's His!

2. Jesus built the foundation of the church (His house), with His blood.

3. The church is an organism not a mere brick and mortar structure. It is made up of people. His house is made up of "believers" worshiping in a building set apart for them to meet in and learn about His kingdom and how to establish it in the earth.

4. Actually, fundamentally, each of us as individual believers, is a house of God. II Corinthians 5:1 says, "If this earthly house of this tabernacle be destroyed we have another building, not made by hand." Then I Corinthians 6:19 says, "Did you not know that your body is the temple of God?"

---

[4] Ibid. 44

5. If we are His house, then we too should be a house of prayer? If we are indeed "God's" holy Temple, then should not prayer be a priority in our lives?

Connecting The Wires

There are some basic things that need to be done to begin the process of becoming a praying Church. The church today has all the wires of the computer, but they aren't connected properly. Therefore, we see power surges, but not stability. Because it is the heart of the father and the lifestyle of the son, then his body should have prayer as a part of their nature, and not something we are dragged into. Here are some suggestions to get your church started:

A. Identify a prayer coordinator/director

B. Build a team- assigning people to pray for specific areas e.g. The lost, marriage, youth, leaders, events in the church

C. Set up training

D. Develop a prayer calendar-monthly prayer targets

E. Search the Internet for national days of prayer and prayer movements

F. Schedule special prayer gatherings

G. For your church -week of prayer

H. Prayer walks through the community -seizing the land- (we did Thursday initiatives on drug corners)

I. Special Night of Prayer for the community - special groups-lead

J. Day of prayer - for the vision of the church

K. Do a citywide prayer event

L. Develop prayer lines for busy people

M. Trainings - National, local and in house conferences (other books By Bishop Husband on prayer that can be used for training: *The Altared Life, I Am The Church and My Name is House of Prayer*)

N. Use Sunday morning as training ground: set Sundays for men, women, youth to lead intercession

Commitments of a Praying Church

We will do nothing without prayer, fasting and reading word of God.

We will help every ministry to have their own prayer leaders that will be committed to keeping them focused.

We will teach regularly the fundamentals of prayer.

We will call our congregations to regular days of prayer.

We will keep local and national prayer initiatives before the church body.

We will regularly join other ministries in praying for their prayer needs.

We will identify intercessors and train them in the area of their passion, so they can be skilled, focused, intentional and successful at their praying posts.

We will create a wall of prayer so that there will be a visible sign that we care for others needs, hurts and dreams.

Back To Basics

One of the problems in the world of sports today, especially when I watch basketball, is the unfortunate reality, that many players are not fundamentally sound. They do not understand the essence of how the game should be played. Basketball, while it may have standout players, is a "team" sport. I have heard recently, one former player say that sports was the great unifier for the "races" or cultures. No matter my pain in hearing that, he made a valid point. We have allowed entertainment to bring us closer together, breaking barriers of color, economics and classes. What a disgraceful, shameful indictment on the church.

When Jesus taught the disciples a model of prayer in Matthew 6, he began by saying "Our" Father". There was no color, culture or economic status attached. When you became His follower, you became His family. So in actuality all of us are related, because all of us were created by the same Father. Some of our siblings have merely surrendered their inheritance in search for soon to be discovered, "deadly worldly pleasures", that appear to be more than they really are.

Rhonda Hughley says, "The house God is building is not a material structure; it is not determined by church tradition or denominational affiliation, particular theology or ethnicity. He is building a new covenant House, where His blood washed people are His temple. The house God's building is simply a unified praying Church… Prayer lies at the very heart of what God is doing and building." [5] I agree with her wholeheartedly, don't you? So then the question must be raised, what are "We" building? This question is raised, because anything contrary to that would be anti-vision, which places us in the "idol building" category. Need I say more?

Jesus raised the statement about prayer and fasting that I think warrants our attention. He said of both of these, "When you ...," Not, "If you ..." The obvious deduction is, that these two disciplines are not optional for us.

You're In The Army Now

Listen my friend. You should be under no illusion, that prayer is not optional. So then, if praying is not an option as a Christian, then we have to decide to go through basic training in order to prepare or equip ourselves for the life in which we are engaged. Author Elizabeth Alves says in her book, *Becoming a Prayer Warrior: A Guide to Effective and Powerful Prayer,* "... Remember, you have an enemy. Ephesians tells us that our struggle is not against flesh and blood, but against the rulers, against the powers, against the world forces of the darkness, against the spiritual forces of wickedness in heavenly places. Ephesians 6:12. You are called to do spiritual warfare through prayer where Satan strongholds are until you win." [6]

Beloved, you are in the Army now! You are either enlisted, or a draftee. If you are a draftee, then more often than not, you would be categorized as a person who is part of the church, but not really certain you want to be "too" seriously involved. You don't mind praying, but you're not certain to what degree of seriousness or intimacy with God you want.

---

[5] Rhonda Hughey, *Desperate for His Presence: God's Design to Transform Your Life and Your City* (Minneapolis, Minn.: Bethany House Publishers, 2004),147,148

[6] Elizabeth Alves, *Becoming a Prayer Warrior: a Guide to Effective and Powerful Prayer*, Revised ed. (Ventura, Calif: Regal, 1998), 32

Come on, if you are truly out of the world, then go after HIM! Get full of God! Take the benefits! Enlisted people walk in continuous hunger. They declare boldly, "I am here". "I signed up for this!" "Where do you want me to be?" "Teach me what I need to learn, so that I can be a lethal weapon against the enemy." "Let's do this!"

Discovering Your DNA

DNA stands for Deoxyribonucleic acid. No wonder they call it DNA! It is a molecule encoding the genetic instructions used in the development and functioning of all known organisms and many viruses. It is very complex and would take many pages, a very good dictionary, and some knowledge of science, biology, chemistry, and physics, to comprehend it in its entirety. However, let's simply say, that it contains the genetic information that allows all modern living things to function, grow and reproduce. Forensic scientists use DNA in the blood, saliva, semen, hair etc. to identify perpetrators of crimes. This is called genetic fingerprinting. It is used as well to discover family relationships.

I have an eye-opening revelation for you. Are you ready? Here it is, "Your DNA matches God's." Okay, calm down. I know you're excited. I am too. We are kin (family). Two things must be determined however:

1. Where do you belong in the body, so your gifts can have the greatest support and impact. (Your spiritual gift assessment)

2. Where is your heart/passion in the area of concern for people, because that's who you will be most apt to pray for consistently.

These are called "lethal weapons training assessments." Finding where and how you work, as well as where and how you pray, are the basic training strategies of spiritual warfare that most Christians bypass and thereby cause weakness in the body.

Intercession

Normally, I would walk through the phases of growth in one's prayer life. I have done that in my three earlier books on prayer: *The Altared Life; Your Body God's Temple; The House Where His Presence Lives; and I Am The Church: And My Name Is House of Prayer*. While they are worth quoting, and the subject is worth repeating, I would rather you buy and read those books and cut to the chase here. I believe if you are reading this book, you already have grown, or are growing past the infant stage, of merely praying for yourself and a few close friends. You are ready to have a heart like God and break out of the box into discovering "Samaria and the uttermost parts…," as you pray.

The Bible encourages our intercession. Intercession, or to intercede, means "to go or pass between; to act between parties with a view to reconcile those who differ or contend; to interpose; to mediate." [7] This is speaking of an attorney type. A representative who stands in the gap for someone who cannot represent themselves properly at a given moment. Your ability and relationship with the judge has merit and allows the case to be heard.

Dutch Sheets powerfully points out in his book on intercessory prayer, that "… Christ's intercession, in keeping with its literal meaning, was not a prayer. He **prayed**, but a work of mediation He did."[8] WOW! In other words He became what He prayed. His life was given to the goal of deliverance

---

[7] http://www.merriam-webster.com/dictionary/intercession Accessed June 14, 2013

[8] Dutch Sheets, *Intercessory Prayer: How God Can Use Your Prayers to Move Heaven and Earth* (Ventura, Calif.: Regal, 2008), 39

of the world. It was not enough to utter the words "Father forgive them…" He decided to be the deciding factor in their forgiveness. Blood was needed, so he gave His. When we pray, do we give ourselves to it as though people's lives depended on our prayer sincerity and passion?

As we go forward you will see in chapter four, a guide to your prayer DNA. We will look at several questions to help you discover where you are and what you should be studying to achieve what I call "marksman" or "expert weapons status". This is the area that frustrates the enemy and excites our DAD!

Just before we deal with that though, I will talk briefly about getting your heart ready to take your city for our King. Let's go Soldier!

Chapter 3 Taking Your City
Step One: Spiritual Mapping

Recently I was at a pastor's retreat and it happened to be during the same week as the (BCS)[9] National College Football Championship Game. One of my friends and colleagues asked me who I thought would win the game. I told him that I was not sure, but that I was hoping Notre Dame would come out victorious over the perennial powerhouse, Alabama Crimson Tide. He then said to me that he was hoping the same but could not see it happening. When I asked why, he said, "coaching." "Coaching?" I responded. And He said, "Yes, coaching is the difference. You cannot give Coach Nick Saban that kind of time to scout out a team and put together a game plan. Given that kind of time, he would put together a plan that will destroy most any team." It is no secret, he was right. Great coaches are not just motivators, but they are skilled at learning their opponent's weaknesses and strengths. They study when and why their opponent does what they do. They study how long have they done what they do and what results have these things caused?

Years ago, Muhammad Ali fought the then indomitable George Foreman. Foreman had pulverized two of Ali's fiercest rivals. Both were early round knockouts by Foreman and both had gone the fight distance with Ali. The odds of Ali winning were slim to none. There was one catch. Ali was a brilliant student of the game and every opponent. He, against the advice

---

[9] Bowl Championship Series

of his team of trainers, used what would famously be called later, "the rope a dope." He knew Foreman did not have the stamina to fight a long fight, so he allowed him to punch himself tired and then after taking punishment and exercising tremendous patience, Ali rose up with a fury of punches and knocked George Foreman out. The knock out was to the surprise of the whole world (Except maybe to Ali).

Reconnaissance

My friend, this is not a game or boxing match. This is war! However, just as sports teams, and boxers have opponents, we too have them in the realm of the spirit. The Kingdom of Light versus the Kingdom of Darkness is a clear and present danger. We can learn valuable lessons from the world of sports, as well as our military, when it comes to battles and strategies for winning.

The word reconnaissance means, "The act of reconnoitering (especially to gain information about an enemy or potential enemy)." Its origin is French. It is an act of surveying, gaining information, and scouting.[10]

In the military there are three types of reconnaissance patrols (be patient, we are going somewhere with this as well): area; zone and route recon teams. Their assignments are to go and pay attention to the territory desire to take over and bring back accurate information on the enemy and the land so a strategy can be formed. Without their intel, success at best, is a shot in the dark. The recon team must have a strong security team, because their mission is dangerous and of utmost importance to victory.

Whether they are looking at one route that is the main road that the enemy travels to supply all of its troops; or the zone or area in which major operations are being done,

---

[10] http://www.merriam-webster.com/dictionary/reconnaissance, Accessed, June 12,2013

weapons stored, "military brass" meets, it takes careful concentration and detail dictation delivered in order to execute to perfection.

Spiritual Mapping

The reason I spent time drawing your attention to sports and the military initially, is because it will now be easier for us to talk clearly about a term that is not new in many "evangelical" or "white" Pentecostal movements. However, it is new terminology to much of the predominately African-American church. The church universal has always been aware that it needed to take notice of its community in order to address its chaos. Yet, taking notice is only touching the "tip of the iceberg." Taking notice does nothing if we're not going to confront the proverbial "elephant in the room." There are issues that every community has, every city has, every state and country has, that needs to be honestly addressed.

Author and prayer strategist George Otis is right, "… community transformation is not an arbitrary event, but rather a product of a cause-and-effect process."[11] He mentions five factors in his book on *Informed Intercession*, that are needed to stimulate this transformation: 1) persevering leadership; 2) fervent united prayer; 3) social reconciliation; 4) public power encounters; and 5) diagnostic research/spiritual mapping. I want to address each of these in reverse order, briefly, as we move forward. It is not my intention to rewrite Otis's book; but to whet your appetite to go out and be an integral part of helping your city experience revival, reconciliation and revelation of righteousness.

---

[11] George Otis Jr, *Informed Intercession* (Ventura, Calif.: Renew, 1999), 55

Treating The Symptoms

A few years ago I went to my doctor to complain about a pain I had in my foot. The pain was excruciating! I limped over from my office at the church. The walk usually takes all of 2 to 3 minutes from door-to-door at a medium pace. This day it required 15 to 20 minutes. I stopped several times along the way to rest. I gritted and groaned. You get the picture. When I finally arrived, my doctor diagnosed what I had as "the rich man's disease "gout. He then went on to tell me that he was prescribing me some medication (that I gladly took to relieve the pain), telling me I would have to take it the rest of my life. That was a bit strong for me. For about a year, of and on, I was taking these pills and they were always accompanied by pain relievers. One day, I grew tired of taking them. I had been praying and confessing that I was healed and would not be on any medication. Then I received a revelation. I decided to research this attack and see what caused gout. I surfed the Internet. I visited health-food stores. I spoke to Naturopathic Doctors. I decided to speak to people about the "ROOT" problems, not just the symptoms. It required some serious work. I eventually had to make some serious changes in me and my eating habits. The end result is a free from medication life.

Spiritual mapping is a plan to get to the root of a community/cities problems so that it can experience deliverance, healing, hope and peace in God. Otis, in *Informed Intercession* (by now you should be putting it on your "to invest in" list), offers three basic questions to help us plan to achieve our goals of transforming our cities: "1) What is wrong with my community?; 2) where did the problem come from?; 3) What can be done to change things?"[12] Here is a list of major areas he addresses in his research. He says, "The first

---

[12] Ibid., 130

thing you want to know about your community is the extent to which the gospel has taken root. Is your town an evangelist's graveyard or a part of a "Bible Belt"? How many Christians worship in the area? What percentage of the population do they represent?" [13] The (six) areas he addresses have these three basic questions interwoven in them.

When Christ is not at the center, bondage is the inevitable result. Cataloging the conditions of pain are a necessary means to an expected end. If we do not see the injustices, the poverty, violence or disease with more than a symptoms treating eye, it will be raised again in this generation and the next following. "Is there NO balm in Gilead to heal the sin sick soul, or to make the wounded whole?" How many liquor stores are there in a community that suffers with alcoholism issues? How has it affected the crime rate?

When all has been said and done God's question to Ezekiel is so appropriate, "Can these bones live?"

Do You See What I See?

Proverbs 29:18 (AMP) says, "Where there is no vision [no redemptive revelation of God], the people perish..." They have no boundaries or standards to live by and thereby they fall for anything and eventually are consumed by death. I believe many people have a limited understanding of what the church is supposed to be and do in the world. We are not mere "innocent bystanders." We are kingdom ambassadors! We are called and sent to bring God's kingdom order in the earth. To do that, we must see the root of every stronghold the enemy of God has in our cities/communities/families and like a heat seeking missile, destroy them. We must see potential, where poverty prevails. We must seek healing, where hurt has become a habit.

---

[13] Ibid.,133

Author and citywide prayer organizer Francis Frangipane notes that we too often see our city's skyline as factories, structures and schools, while Jesus is seeing the people. He says, "Yes, the eyes of the Lord probe the spirit and humanity of the city. From his eternal perspective He also beholds the most terrible event known to man. He sees the overwhelming horror, the utter despair an unsaved soul experiences as he realizes he is, indeed, dead and going to hell. And in the midst of it all, He sees the church, His church, purchased at the cost of His own precious blood-sitting comfortably, remote control in hand, watching television."[14]

I call that being spiritually "mapped" as opposed to spiritual "mapping." The enemy is doing recon as well. Don't ever forget that! His job is to make the abnormal normal for us and the normal (Kingdom life) appear abnormal, so that we will abdicate our responsibilities here. I agree with Frangipane, that the church needs to be cleansed of its visionless, loveless relationship to its cities. We too often have become what I have mentioned in other writings, "incestuously religious" (lovers of ourselves, our fellowship). We are taught by Jesus to love our neighbors, the lost, and our enemies; praying for them all. In our time of prayer we are to seek strategies for their reconciliation to us, one another and the FATHER. He keeps asking us over and over, "Do You See What I See?" Our answer must be a resounding, Yes!

Turf War

I have pastored in the inner city for over 30 years. It has been both rewarding and very challenging. At inconvenient times the latter makes every effort to convince me that the former is not worth it... But God. One of the continual issues in any inner city is a battle of people over what they call "their

---

[14] Francis Frangipane, *The House of the Lord: God's Plan to Liberate Your City from Darkness* (Lake Mary, Fla.: Charisma House, 1996), 81

turf." Strangely enough, in very few instances, do any of them own the land they are fighting and dying over. Tragic stories of senseless death are a weekly occurrence that may be met with tears, but often doesn't turn into transformation. Why?

I want to offer two reasons:

1. We often do not attach social ills to spiritual problems. Therefore we try to legislate it with man-made laws, locking down neighborhoods, and locking away nuisances with names, for life. Granted, we have people in our society of every culture who are incorrigible. It is their choice. However, rarely do we put together a comprehensive plan to do preventative care for cities, that include serious spiritual mapping, prayer walks, and community prayer days. When do we invest in that side of community planning? When we are going in to renovate a public housing area, how do we do that without addressing root issues that cause generations to settle there and call it a home worth fighting for and dying over?

2. Our leaders are often at war themselves. They are either in a political war, so they cannot value one another enough to discover the common good for the people they have been called to serve, or they are at war within themselves for self significance, so they must chase personal dreams, goals, positions and of course money.

This is why our real leaders MUST be intercessors or our intercessors must be our real leaders. We must see prayer as a driving force of transformation in our cities. Declare right now that your name is Elijah (in the spirit). There will be no rain until you say so! Your intercession is the key to breaking turf wars in the public housing and public/local government, where Democrats and Republicans are as bad as those fighting and killing one another in the "hood" over turf that they do not own. Decide today, that for the rest of your life, you will lead where you live and that your leading will begin with interceding.

Team G. A. S.

In the church where I have been privileged to serve, after years of hitting and missing when it comes to a strategy for building healthy successful events, and ministries, I designed something called our "pyramid of success."

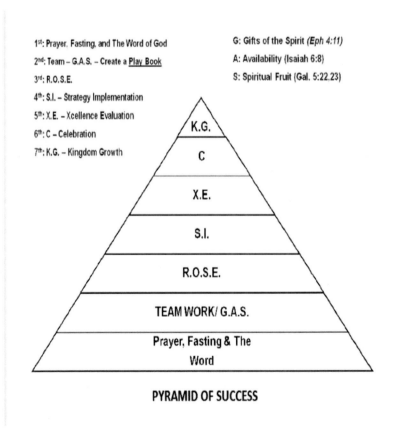

1st: Prayer, Fasting, and The Word of God
2nd: Team – G.A.S. – Create a Play Book
3rd: R.O.S.E.
4th: S.I. – Strategy Implementation
5th: X.E. – Xcellence Evaluation
6th: C – Celebration
7th: K.G. – Kingdom Growth

G: Gifts of the Spirit *(Eph 4:11)*
A: Availability (Isaiah 6:8)
S: Spiritual Fruit (Gal. 5:22,23)

PYRAMID OF SUCCESS

The bottom, foundation of everything is prayer, fasting and the Word of God. We do not do anything unless it has this at its base. The next level is what I want to talk with you about. It is called "Team G. A. S." It involves building a team of *Gifted, Available* people who exercise *Spiritual* fruit. If they are gifted and unavailable, they can't help achieve an end. If they are available but not gifted, they waste your time because although you may teach them to perform things, it is not done with the excellence as it would be if they were gifted. If the gift and the availability are working and the people do not exercise spiritual fruit (Galatians 5:22, 23), then longevity in success is not likely to take place. While they may finish a project, they will often not desire to work together again. The idea then, is to get the right people in the right places at the right time to plan, to pursue, execute, evaluate, restructure if needed, and finish with God being glorified every time. Then, when they come out of one event, they look forward to the next time they will have an opportunity to work together. At least that is the idea (or ideal).

John Dawson of Youth With A Mission said, "Identify your city's prophets, intercessors and spiritual elders. In every city there is what I call a hidden eldership-a group of saints that you will not find listed in any book. It consists of God's Circle of mature believers who "stand in the gap" until victory comes... Some of these watchmen are obvious, such as veteran pastors. Others may be intercessors in obscurity or prophetic people with a premonition. If there is a common theme among those who are sensitive to the spirits guidance, you're onto something."[15]

Dawson encourages us to study our cities demographics and ask basic questions we have posed earlier in this chapter. Where do the people live and why? How many of them are in poverty and why? What are the cultural dynamics in the

---

[15] C. Peter Wagner, *Territorial Spirits: Practical Strategies for How to Crush the Enemy through Spiritual Warfare* (Shippenburg, PA: Destiny Image, 2012), 165

neighborhoods? Are they changing? What causes unrest? What are the one or two hot bed issues of the people? Who is addressing them?

Ground Zero
(Richmond, VA. In Particular)

We're getting ready to strategically divide our forces for battle. But first I want to tell you how I came to write this book and this chapter specifically. I believe that our nation has a serious stronghold in the area of discrimination. For years I believed that it was merely a color issue. Hatred, racism, discrimination is a demonic seed in the earth. However, at its root, may be greed, and the love of money.

I believe the seed of racism in America began in Virginia. Therefore, the seed of reconciliation must begin there (here where I have lived for 33 years). Virginia is a strategic spiritual battleground because of its history and cannot be overlooked as the mother territory of a nation. For years I pastored here without understanding why I remained. I had a good old traditional church and I was just glad to be preaching and earning a living. That all changed at my personal "Ground Zero."

One definition of Ground Zero is, "the center or origin of intense or violent activity or change." It is generally a watermark event. Every life has them. Every ministry/business experiences them. You should be at the forefront of the making of a "Ground Zero" happen (spiritually), in your city. At the altar of our church, I had an awakening. Through fasting and praying and serious soul-searching, I discovered my God and myself. This was a second touch experience. It was a recall; a rebirthing. This began the journey to my purpose. I saw the experiences I have had with "racial discrimination" as a springboard to transform a city that would transform a nation. I recognized a life affected by a mother who worked to educate and raise up challenged inner-city youth and a father who was often the lone person of color in his management consultant firm. Both spectrums inform my life today in ministry. My personal spiritual mapping enabled me to locate the place of my effectiveness. It helped me understand *me* so that I could fulfill my divine purpose.

The Journey Begins

I finally took a class at Richmond Hill, (a prayer retreat center), so I could now learn about the history of the city in which I lived and pastored. Wow, this is 20 some years after I started pastoring. What a huge gap of time has gone by! That class alone helped me view races/cultures differently. It helped me see poverty differently and why it persists. It helped me see neighborhoods differently and how they were strategically divided. I began to look at the educational system and the economic fathers of the city. I learned about the difference ways of thinking between those who lived on opposite sides of the river and why they rarely crossed sides of town. I learned about the James River and the canals in downtown Richmond where slave trading was done. All of these things help to inform my prayer life and my preaching/teaching.

Your city has its own unique DNA. Do not allow the enemy to know more about the church in your city and their flaws/failures, than you know about "his" disruptions in the communities where you are called by God to give oversight and have dominion. Your city needs your commitment. Draw a new map in your city with character as its boundaries and God at its center. Make every destination lead to Him. Bring back the church as the center of life. Become Abraham for your city and intercede. Plead on its behalf.

Well, it's time! It's time for you to see specifically, where you fit in. Over the rest of the chapters in this book, you will learn your special place in the intercessory prayer body, so you can effectively/strategically bring transformation/revival to your city. I am in it with you and await to hear of your success. Let's do this!

Chapter 4 Entrance Exam

I remember graduating from grade school (8th grade) and preparing to go to high school. There were two choices before me. One was a public high school where my girlfriend was attending and the other was a private (all boys) college prep school. I had to take an entrance exam to both schools. The public school was obviously my first choice and I passed the exam excitedly expecting to attend the school. On the other hand, what I did not know, was that there was one thing/person working against my plan from taking place. First, let me inform you that I also passed the exam to the private school, but there was a catch to it. To be accepted there, I had to attend summer school. No brainer, right? School with my girl friend here I come. Of course I was unwilling to go to summer school to attend an all boy's school and I let it be known as I protested to the point of tears. I however failed in my protests, because I had not factored in the one variable that mattered most. You see, my father knew more about me and where I needed to be than I did. He had also given me an exam. He watched my life with careful loving scrutiny and determined that the best school for me would be the all-male school. It would require me to do extra study. It would force me to concentrate on my life and purpose and not be distracted (by my girlfriend or girls period, as it was for much of my seventh and eighth grade years). Thank God for my dad's wisdom. While I was still not finished with that issue in my life when I graduated, those four years could have proven to be a destructive disastrous period in my pursuit of purpose.

Why am I telling you this story? It is because you need to know that your "FATHER" knows best, Always! Not always your natural father, but your heavenly Father, will always be watching and directing you to your proper place, to fulfill His purpose for your life.

This chapter is designed to be that *entrance exam* to the "school of prayer." After taking the exam, you will then discover the area your FATHER wants you to concentrate in so that you become the most effective intercessor possible. When you finish the exam, you should know your number one(1) and two (2) place of passion that you should be studying in this book. The other chapters are good reference writings as well, as referral material when you meet people in other areas of the intercessory prayer symphony (body). Read them and be informed.

Gifts vs. Passions

Spiritual gifts are "special instruments God gives us for the unique tasks of the church, that help us carry out a special task; bringing people to God."[16] They are "evidence or a demonstration that God's Holy Spirit is working in us, enabling us to do things we could otherwise not do."[17] While I agree that is His gift in us and that we could or would not be able to do it without His enabling, I also recognize that we have a choice. We can choose to recognize a gift and do nothing with it. We could also choose to recognize and except that we have it, then use it for our own glory. It is a beautiful thing, when all of the people in a ministry are in concert with one another, using their God-given gifts (ability) to achieve His purpose.

---

[16] Jane A.G. Kise, David, Stark, Sandra Krebs Hirsh, *LifeKeys,* Minneapolis, Minn: Bethany House Publishers, 61

[17] Ibid., 62

What is different about intercession, is that even though it may indeed be a call, the areas we are called into "are" passion driven. Passion is defined as "a strong liking or enthusiasm for a subject or activity".[18] As you will discover shortly there will be some areas of intercession you will be drawn to more than others. Learn to feed your passion and pursue it. You should have a burden for *at least* one area or two, without being burdened in a negative way. For instance, in ministry, I have a burden for teaching and preparing leaders. I really do not enjoy hospital visitations. I do them. I can be good at ministering to the people there. However, it is not a place of passion for me. It is a different burden This one refers to a burden like a load being carried. The burden I have for teaching/preaching helping churches and pastors is one that makes my life unfulfilled if I do not exercise it. They are two different kinds of burdens. Consequently, I get others to do more of the hospital visitations, because they feel called to do it. As a result, they do it with joy and do it well. It doesn't mean I do not care about the sick! My passion and gifting is in other areas and I should not feel bad to pursue my passions and exercise my areas. However, there are times I am called on and gladly go (to hospitals, nursing homes). You can operate anywhere for a time, but you operate best where you have passion.

Find your passion place in intercession and pursue it. You will spend the least effort, barely knowing how long you have been interceding, in the area which your passion lies.

Okay, Get Your Pencils Ready!

As you prepare to take this entrance exam, hear the words of noted pastor, professor, and prolific lecturer, George Buttrick, who said in a writing on Intercessory prayer, " If you

---

[18] http://www.merriam-webster.com/dictionary/passion, Accessed June 17,2013

were to ask the man on the street, Do you believe in Intercessory prayer? He might echo blankly, 'intercessory?' If you were then to explain that theology is fond of long words and that you meant prayer on behalf of other people, he might answer in a silent skepticism. Even among church folk the sea of faith is at the ebb. Behold the intercessor. He kneels in some church to pray for our chaotic world. He pleads divine protection for his son who, let us suppose is a newspaper correspondent in England or China. There he kneels- alone so far as eyes can see. What can he do? Can he stay this natural calamity or that national aggression? If a shell should fall on London, can he shield his son? To our skeptical sight the intercessor may be a lovable and even a saintly figure, but he is pathetic and futile."[19]

My dear friend, you are neither pathetic nor futile. You "are" Jesus in the earth, misunderstood, but nevertheless effecting what the eyes are not always privileged to see. So PRAY WITHOUT CEASING!

"Your *prayers* are getting ready to shape the world!"

---

[19] George Arthur Buttrick, *Prayer,* New York-Nashville: Abingdon-Cokesbury Press, 96

Chapter 5 The Worship Intercessor

By now you have an inclination that this is a passion area for you. I want to welcome you to my personal intercession passion place. While I believe that all of the places in this orchestra of intercession are vital to the tearing down of strongholds and returning unrealized dominion to the body of Christ, I am convinced that this is the key that unlocks the door to all others. Psalm 100:4 says, *"Enter into His gates with thanksgiving, and into His courts with praise"* (KJV). The conversation starter in prayer begins with the heart that is appreciative that it has an audience and acknowledges that gratitude, with verbal observations, of which are intended to exalt.

Magnify Him

When I was growing up, there used to be little gifts in boxes of this caramel corn box, called "Cracker Jacks". Ok, so they still have Cracker Jacks, it's been a long time since I had some, so I don't know if they still have prizes inside. Anyway, stop distracting me (smile). Inside of one of those boxes was something I began to play with and then studied a little about. It was called a "magnifying glass". Of course the toy was plastic, but in time I learned the significance of it. It had at least two uses: (1) It was used to make what you were looking at larger; and (2) it could also be used, if you allowed the sun or light to shine through it, to burn that which was under it.

When you magnify God, you enlarge Him above everything in the earth realm. You make Him bigger and everything else smaller. In essence, you are ascribing a worth to God that far exceeds anything else. Nothing in earth compares to Him. Your love for Him and appreciation for Him draws you to spend time, intimate quality time with Him, that in the end begins to make you and all around you look like Him.

Magnifying Him also allows the SON to shine through you, burning up the things of this world that seek to steal your attention and detour your destiny. You cannot fully devote yourself to two loves. His love demands exclusivity. Either your magnifying of Satan will burn up your passion/love for God or the other way around. Too often we see a sad battle of internal warfare because believers will not loose themselves completely, from the world. This internal warfare is a great cause of the problems that exist in the world. You cannot fight a legitimate, strong war, on two fronts. An old adage says you can't build a city and fight a war at the same time. No wonder Jesus said, you must "Worship the Lord thy God and Him only" (Matthew 4:10)

All of Me

Dick Eastman says "Worship is any act, thought or expression of willful adoration that exalts and enthrones God, thereby defeating and dethroning Satan. When intercession that is prayerful intervention in the needs of others is added, we have intercessory worship". [20] James Goll, noted writer in this area of Worship in his book on *"The Lost Art of Practicing the Presence"*, describes worship in the chapters on Extravagant Worship, as something we do with our whole being, not just our tongues. Often, we speak of worship as a practice of the tongue and not the heart. We make claims that a person is a

---

[20] Dick Eastman, *Intercessory Worship: Combining Worship and Prayer to Touch the Heart of God* (Ventura, Calif: Regal, 2012), 21

worship leader or a worshipper, because of ability/talent and not enough based upon submission to the Holy Spirit.

Goll writes, "Worship involves your entire being – heart, mind, will, and emotions. Much of what we have called worship in the past has been nothing more than stale religiosity. Extravagant worship, on the other hand involves total abandonment of our will, a total consciousness of what we are doing as we express our deep love for God in the complete thrusting of ourselves upon Him in rapturous expressions of love and joy and adoration".[21]

When we enter His presence without inhibitions, our soul (mind, will, emotions) body, and spirit at His disposal, ANYTHING is possible. You see, I believe that worship has these phases:

1. We acknowledge and appreciate His kindness towards us.

2. We declare who He is and is becoming in and through us

3. He comes near as we call Him

4. We come face to face with Him and we see ourselves in contrast

5. There is a weeping that cleanses any pretensions

6. We refocus and we see Him clearly and begin to see ourselves like He is

7. Intimacy / Oneness happens

---

[21] James Goll *The Lost Art of Practicing His Presence*, (Destiny Image Shippensburg PA 2005), 83

8. Pregnancy is produced

9. We begin to talk like Him and to Him in a back and forth love language

10. Infused/Impregnated with His Spirit, we pray/intercede in love for others

11. Atmospheres are shifted as we call His name and others

12. Witnesses in the room or nearby are transformed

He Started It

When God came here, He became the example (through Jesus) of extravagant love. He set a standard of love that was without precedent. He left everything in Glory without a word of complaint, and gave His body to us as a sacrifice. He said, "It's yours and I will do anything to prove to you I love you. I will die to every emotion, thought, and will. I determine to give all of Me, for all of you. I am your worship intercessory seed. When I finish, you will have a model that you can follow, for eternity. As a matter of fact, I will be your model "in" eternity. I will never stop interceding for you.

Dick Eastman says "The term intercessory worship, I believe, refers to concentrated, passionate "worship saturated prayer" that rises with the fragrance of incense before Gods throne. In response, God releases His power to accomplish His purposes for the Harvest.

> And when He had taken it, the four living creatures and the twenty-four elders fell down before the Lamb. Each one had a harp and they were holding golden bowls full of incense,

which are the prayers of the saints. And they sang a new song: "You are worthy to take the scroll and to open its seals, because You were slain, and with Your blood You purchased men for God from every tribe and every language and people and nation. You have made them to be a Kingdom and priests to serve our God, and they will reign on the earth."
When He opened the seventh seal, there was silence in heaven for about half an hour. And I saw the seven angels who stand before God, and to them were given seven trumpets. Another angel, who had a golden censer, came and stood at the altar. He was given much incense to offer, with the prayers of all the saints, on the golden altar before the throne. The smoke of the incense, together with the prayers of the saints, went up before God from the angel's hand then the angel took the censer, filled it with fire from the altar, and hurled it on the earth; and there came peals of thunder, rumblings, flashes of lightening and an earthquake. Then the seven angels who had the seven trumpets prepared to sound them. (Revelation 5:8-10; 8:1-6 NIV)

Interestingly, the Worshippers coming before the lamb with harps (symbols of worship) in one hand and bowls (symbols of prayers and intercession) in the other to combine these two symbols in a song never sung before."[22]

---

[22] Eastman, *Intercessory Worship*, 19

Knock Knock, Whose There?

The timeless game "Knock knock whose there" has always been a favorite pass time of mine that produced laughter. It is especially fun with my young children. They never get tired of it and come up with the funniest "whose there" lines ever. Or how about the prank game some kids play (called knock down ginger – dating back to the 19th century) where they knock on a door or ring someone's doorbell and run away before the person can answer? Well, the kids enjoy that game much more than adults do, I assure you. Have you ever considered that prayer is a kind of knocking on heaven's door? Like knock, knock, whose there, our dad gets excited that He hears our knock and with joyous anticipation He comes to answer us. On the other hand, how disappointed He is when He arrives to entertain us, and we have decided to play a game of run and hide. The question you are raising now is, how is it that I can be praying and hiding at the same time? Have you considered that many people spend their time in prayer as a ritual, religious practice without truly offering their heart to God in the process? You see, when you come knocking, see if Heaven shows up at the gate/door. He comes and readies everything at your disposal. He is expecting all of you, which includes your faith and love for Him and others.

Intercessors who are in the Worship section of the orchestra/body should always approach God with ALL of themselves filled with the fruit of the Spirit ready to be poured out for Him, on behalf of others. Seeing the reflection of Himself excites Him. Whenever you knock, know that it's not a game, lives are at stake and **you** are the key that unlocks the chain to their freedom. You open the gate!

Behind the Door

There is a game show that originally aired on television in the 1950's, and is still on the air today, called "The Price Is

Right". I used to watch it with my grandmother and still remember the excitement building as people would stand there contemplating whether they would choose what was behind door number one, two, or three. The crowd would be yelling frantically on the set of the show and we would be doing the same in granny's bedroom. Often, people would choose the wrong door and the prize would be pigs, or a cow, or something really funny and often useless. There were other times the right choice would be made and the prize was special and worth quite a bit. Each contestant stood there anxiously awaiting to see what was behind the door they chose. They were expecting special.

You my dear friend are an intercessor. You are also a worshipper. You too stand at the door/gate of glory. Your heart has been poured out to God. You have lavishly "wasted" your life on the feet of Christ as a sweet fragrance. Let me tell you very assuredly, there will be NO disappointments behind the door. You can expect at least four things:

- New Songs – He will give you songs, as you sing songs to Him. Do not be concerned about your key/ notes/ melody, have the sound of heaven.

- Revelation of Relationship – You cannot sow intimacy without receiving the same. God will begin to reveal Himself to you in greater measures and increase your capacity for/ to love.

- Release of Authority – With relationship (Him in you) comes responsibility. You are His ambassador in the earth. You open up the heavens and release the power of praise and the understanding of the power of His presence. You also place in subjection the realms of darkness. You put demons in check. Worship makes you look like, act like God. It's His fueling station and that fuel infuriates as well as defuses the enemy. When Satan asked Jesus to worship Him in Matthew 4, he was asking Him to trade camps. He said in essence, "become me", abandon ship." Jesus' answer caused Satan to run from Him "for a season". Your intercessory worship filled life, will cause Satan to STAY angry with you and keep his distance.

- Harvest – Righteousness; Peace; Joy in the Holy Spirit; Angelic Help, working to manifest what you are interceding about.

The Offering

Often in scripture we find scriptures that deal with worship corresponding to or in congruency with giving. It is consistent because, again, the very root of worship has to deal with "worth". Luke 12:34 says to us, "For where your treasure is, there your heart will be also." You invest in what is most significant to you. You put your money, time and effort there. God judges the heart of our gifts, not the amounts. The first real act of worship is seen in Genesis 4. Abel out "hearted" Cain with the gift he gave to God. He determined the worth of God in his heart and gave a gift that he felt would best represent that. He gave the best offering he had. That was an act of worship.

Abraham changed the game. He redefined the definition of worship. Or maybe we should merely say that he raised the standard. This time God asked him for an offering. He willingly brought his only son to an altar of sacrifice. This is the son that took him 20 years of patience to receive. Now God says to him, "offer him to me as a sacrifice in worship."

Jesus raised the bar even more. He decided to give himself as an offering. This is the essence of worship intercession. "I offer my consecrated life as a fragrance before you Lord. I come as a dead man before you on behalf of others, that my death will be a sacrifice for their sins and give them life." It is what Paul was saying to the Church at Rome. "Therefore I urge you, brothers, in view of God's mercy, to offer your bodies as living sacrifices, holy and pleasing to God – this is your spiritual act of worship." Romans 12:2 (NIV)

Intruders Beware

False worship is dangerous. It is in essence trying to gain unlawful entrance. First of all, God knows our hearts and we cannot fool him. Secondly, people are disappointed because "hoopla" took place, but nothing opened and nothing was broken. Thirdly, when we damage God's people, we must be held accountable to Him. All false worship is not merely the worship of *obvious* idols. Some false worship is an *art* form and not easily detectable. It is "strange fire to our God. It is what I call "crowd performance" or "show time" worship. It is motivated by people, not a relationship with God.

Simon the sorcerer in Acts 8:9-21, 22, wanted to purchase the power of the Holy Spirit because he liked the affects it had on others and the popularity it produced. The Seven Sons of Sceva in Acts 19:8-20 used the name of Jesus, intruding on spiritual turf that they had no heart for. Their father was a priest, so they learned the language, but their hearts were still captured by the enemy. When it was said and done, the enemy said, "You can't act like you love God and me too." I will not let you keep getting away with cheating on me." So he exposed them. Intruders BEWARE! Don't forget, Satan was a worship leader.

Building An Altar

1 Chronicles 21:26 says, "David built an altar to the Lord there and sacrificed burnt offerings and fellowship offerings. He called on the LORD, and the LORD answered him with fire from heaven on the altar of burnt offerings."

Genesis 12:7 says, "The LORD appeared to Abram and said, "To your offspring I will give this land." So he built an altar there to the LORD". With Abraham particularly this act became a habit (Genesis 12:8; 13:4; 13:18; 22:9). He passed this habit down to his son Isaac (Genesis 26:25). Altars were sacred places of remembrance and sacrifice where people often returned to connect with God. It was a place where there was an exchange taking place between God and his prized creation; a place where man offers God something and God gives back. Literally, altar means, "a place of slaughter sacrifice" in the Hebrew language. They were made of different things; unhewn stone; wood-fig; walnut and pine. One was for a lasting remembrance as a statue, the other to burn sacrifices upon as an offering.

We are the Altar today! We are the place of sacrifices. We are the place people should experience God and remember Him for who He is, what He is doing, what He has done, and shall do in the earth. Our lives are the place where atmosphere is created for worshipping Him.

Example of Worship Intercession

The writers of the book "Intercession" give us incite in this area. "Worship Intercessors are the ones who release the cannons of faith against the walls of resistance. They carry spiritual artillery for breakthrough."[23]

Moses worshipped with the people of God after crossing the Red Sea. (Wouldn't you have as well?)

Joshua, who became an intercessor on his face, while Moses was in the tent of meeting talking with God, eventually led worship intercession around the walls of Jericho.

David troubled Saul with his worship intercession.

---

[23] Elizabeth (Beth) Alves and Barbara (Tommi) Femrite & Karen Kaufman, *Intercessors* (Ventura, Calif.: Regal, 2000), 179

Jehoshaphat stirred up the heavens and ambushed the enemy by praise and worshipping God in the face of an enemy that was notorious for cutting off the heads of its enemy as a fear factor for the next victims to behold.

Alves and company conclude, "In each of these situations, three common threads intertwine to form a sturdy cord for hauling in the breakthrough: sacrifice, sanctification and surrender. Worship intercession that ushers in God's presence must have all three- and cultivating those character traits always takes time. Remember: Spiritual growth is a process."[24]

Many of the Psalms are examples of Worship intercession. Take time to use these four for your prayer time today: Psalm 92; Psalm 93; Psalm 138; Psalm 145. Each of these will call for you to speak well of Him, declaring His goodness and opening His heart for a time of supplication.

Tools that *Enhance* the Experience

It has been my experience in this area that you must be careful to use the right vessels to usher in His presence. Motives are major! I want to list some other ingredients that will help with your altar building (a place God feels welcome to come). Remember, again, This is NOT a show!

1. He doesn't mind dancing with you, so dance

2. He appreciates your words of thanks and signs of His Name posted in the room

3. An opportunity to bring a gift of significance before Him (Especially if it's just your surrendered heart or

---

[24] Alves, *Intercessors*, 180

an area heretofore separated from or for Him.

4. Music – Strategic – Not always words to it, but Heart Provoking Music – Music that causes concentration on Him. Words and Music together help, as long as they are not distracting, like a favorite song that causes you to think about your choir, church, recording project.... *"That's my song,"* is undoubtedly not what you want to be concentrating on while you are with Him.

5. Confessions / Proclamation / Affirmations-speaking His Word back to Him is delightful to His ears, as well as faith developing for you

6. REPENTANCE- Cleansing is critical to real worship. Psalm 24:3, 4 says, "Who may climb the mountain of the LORD? Who may stand in his holy place? Only those whose hands and hearts are pure, who do not worship idols"

7. Other Worshippers (if this is a corporate effort) – You can always lead the intercession. Other worshippers help set the atmosphere for breakthrough waiting to take place as well. Alone, know this: "One man of you shall chase a thousand, for the LORD your God is He who fights for you, as He promised you." (Joshua 23:10 KJV)

Some of Today's Worship Intercessors
(These may help ignite something in you)

Bishop William Murphy
Eddie James
Misty Edwards
Terry MacAlmon

Jason Upton
Kim Walker
Heidi Baker

Books to Feed Your Passion

Intercessory Worship by Dick Eastman
Worship Warrior by Chuck Pierce with John Dickson
Practicing His Presence by James Goll
Hosting His Presence by Bill Johnson
Desperate for His Presence by Rhonda Hughley

Chapter 6 The Prophetic Intercessor And The Watchman Anointing

Welcome to the team of prophetic intercessors! Of course, if you are merely a student of intercession and are reading this chapter because you want to increase your learning, then I applaud you for your interest. One way or the other, let's get started in helping you see this critical area of intercession. As we mentioned in an earlier chapter, each area of this band of intercessors is vitally important to the body of Christ as it seeks to fulfill its purpose in the earth. The prophetic intercessor has a lifesaving anointing on them. They must never take lightly the call upon their lives.

Paying Attention to the Inner Voice

Have you ever been in a conversation with someone, or in a classroom, and the information being given out was important, but your mind was somewhere else? The person talking to you, maybe a teacher, seeing your demeanor says, "Are you paying attention?" Or, "Are you listening to me?" Suppose it is your teacher or your boss and the information being given will be on a test later? Suppose it is a part of an important assignment that could cost your employer money or even worse, what if it could cost peoples' lives? Always know who you are and how important your life is, so that you do not miss information that potentially will help you and others.

Just as your outer ears are important to listen to natural voices, the news, spiritual and secular leaders, etc., so too is your inner ear critical. The ability to hear beyond words, is an area that all intercessors, especially prophetic ones, need to develop. God does not merely speak to us through people, He also speaks to people *through* us. Therefore, we must pay attention to the *"inner voice"*.

Cindy Jacobs shares an amazing story which illustrates the importance of paying attention to the inner voice and the power of prophetic intercession. She writes:

> "When a team from Frontline Ministries landed in Guatemala City, Guatemala, they felt anticipation for the task ahead as they went into the city to stay for the night. Among the team members was our good friend Dutch Sheets. He and others had come to build a ministry center in Penten Jungle on the Passion River. Little did they know that they were stepping into a situation in which their lives depended on the obedience of an intercessor from Ohio named Linda Snelling, who was aware of the trip. The group arrived on a Friday night planning to fly out on Saturday to their ministry destination in the jungle the next morning. Dutch went to the airport and found that their flight had been canceled. For those of you who are not familiar with travel in Central America, this is not unusual. The airport authorities simply told them that they would have to come back on Sunday. The team went to pray, asking the Lord for his direction. Was Satan trying to keep them from leaving, or did God want them to stay in the city one more night? Finally, the group in Guatemala felt that they should try to leave and negotiated back and forth with the Guatemalan Airlines representatives. Meanwhile, back in Ohio, Linda Snelling was on her knees.

For over three hours she agonized in prayer for the team. She prayed and prayed until finally she received a release from God. This prayer helped turn the stony heart of the airline people; suddenly, for no reason, after three hours of arguing, they change their minds, through up their hands and said, "Get on the plane. We will fly you now."

The next morning at 3 AM one of the worst earthquakes in the history of the nation hit Guatemala City. It killed 30,000 people and left 1 million homeless. When the team returned from the jungle they went to the hotel and homes where they had stayed the previous Friday night and would have been on Saturday night. To their shock they discovered that many of them would have been crushed to death had they stayed that second night when the ceilings fell in and beams landed on top of the very beds in which they would have slept. How they praise God for his intervention and grace. When they returned, Dutch heard about Linda Snelling's prophetic intercession on their behalf, and a sense of wonder filled his heart along with gratitude. His amazement increased when he found out that she prayed during the exact three-hour period when they were in the midst of negotiations with the Guatemalan Airlines representatives. Thank God for the **extra** team member God sent with the Frontline team! And thank God for a faithful prayer warrior who said, "Here I am Lord, send me; I will go on my knees." We may never know how much work for the kingdom of God was affected by her prayers" [25]

Defining the Term

The word prophetic has its obvious root in the word prophecy. Peter Wagner says, "The gift of prophecy is the special ability that God gives to certain members of the Body of Christ to receive and communicate an immediate message of God to His people through a divinely anointed utterance." [26] I think that is well said. It then would hold every prophet accountable for not only speaking that word into the lives of others, but also praying for it to be received and coming to God's expected end. The prophet Jonah is the perfect case study for what you cannot do as a privileged recipient of this grace. He received God's word for Nineveh and neither prays for the city nor obediently runs to broadcast the message. He is severely dealt with because of it.

Again, intercession means to literally stand in the gap for someone or a group of persons. It is having the responsibility of being a representative on their behalf, with a "higher court." Because of the relationship the intercessor has with God, he or she has a right to go to Him on behalf of another for their benefit. Their relationship with the one, or both parties, is critical to the outcome.

Combining the Terms

Remember that prophecy is both foretelling and forth-telling. It in other words is both; predicting that which is to come; and declaring revelation about what you heard/hear. You *see*, then you *say*. You *hear*, then you *share*. It is voicing

---

[25] Cindy Jacobs, *Possessing the Gates of the Enemy: A Training Manual For Militant Intercession*, (Chosen Books: Grand Rapids, Michigan 1994) 145, 146

[26] C. Peter Wagner, *Your Spiritual Gifts Can Help Your Church Grow* (Regal Books Glendale CA 1979) 228

vision, as well as *helping* people envision, what God has voiced.

Pieces to the Puzzle

The prophetic intercessor is made up of a certain character. They have seven pieces of a puzzle that make them whole:

1. They have a heart that is sold out to God and His will to be done in the earth.

2. They love God's people – Notice that I said, they are, "God's" people. Remember that always, even when they do not act like it. That's why *you* are in their lives.

3. They have a desire to see the people they prophesy over, live out their created worth. They believe, like Moses, in the destiny of the people and tirelessly, prophetically will them to their promised place.

4. Their ears are always open to hear God's plan of "Destruction or Direction."

5. They speak the message to people in expectation of transformation. Their speaking is not influenced by the people's actions, but by the voice of God alone.

6. They pray diligently until…telling God's plans constantly. They understand that prayer is their own fuel to endure, when deaf ears are apparent in their midst.

7. They see this assignment as urgent as eating, drinking and sleeping. It is life for them. "Prophetic Intercession is not something an intercessor conjures up; it is a choice to surrender to the heartbeat of God in prayer. It

is the result of nestling your ear up against His heart to hear the things that cause Him hurt, happiness, frustration – all the emotions that we feel. As we lay aside our own agendas for His sake in prayer, we can expect to encounter the spirit of prophecy for the people, places and situations that He wants to speak to through our intercession."[27]

With almost all of the other areas of intercession, there comes a time when we rely on what our physical eyes have seen, ears have heard, data collected etc., to give foundation and direction for our prayer time. However, worship and prophetic intercession always begins with the internal calling, to transform the external. He uses our time in prayer, our time of sleep (dreams), and also interrupts daily activity (day dreams), so He can call our attention to a need He wants addressed. Here again is why the prophetic intercessor must be sold out, have an open invitation, open door policy, permission ALWAYS granted, for God to speak *or* paint (pictures before our eyes).

Priceless Treasure

There is a show that comes on television that my wife, her mom and sisters like to watch (I am not a big T.V. guy outside of some sports and black and white movies), called "Pawn Stars", where people bring all these artifacts they have found in their garages, grandparents houses, estate sales etc., to see if they have any real value. She twisted my arm to watch it a couple of times and we both sat guessing the worth of every item. Some things we learned were: (1) Don't judge things by their appearance; (2) Don't under estimate the value of *old* things; (3) If you want to know the value of something, take it

---

[27]Alves *Intercessors,* 235

to an expert; and finally, (4) It may take time to investigate the item, so be patient with the process.

As prophetic intercessors, you are given old, seemingly outdated words, principles, morals and truths to hold. What you have must never be underestimated in value. You can never allow the world to place its worth on life. Only God can tell you what a life is worth. You are holding priceless treasure in your mouth. What you say has the potential to change cities and even a nation. With so great a treasure, there is a tremendous need for the prophetic intercessor to carry certain strong attributes: (1) patience; (2) faith; and (3) grace.

Protecting The Treasure

1. Patience

Prophetic Intercessors must know that the word they are carrying may take years to manifest. God, does not always have His word manifest immediately and therefore time passes before we experience change. Jeremiah was so discouraged by the people that he wanted to quit preaching. Know that you are the messenger, not the time keeper. Do your job and let God do His. It took 20 years for Abraham and Sarah to see the pregnancy promised them. Great seeds for great harvests may take several seasons to come to maturity.

2. Faith

Patience is an ingredient in Faith. Believing that God knows what He is doing even when we cannot see the sense in continuing, is critical. Understand this, from the process of a seed. One has to begin by knowing the seed *is* going to produce. We then plant it, understanding that it will require time and patience to see the end result. We water and keep weeds away, because we believe something is coming. We never put bricks or anything where the seeds are planted that will hinder their coming forth, because we expect, have faith (even though we cannot see anything yet), that the seed *WILL* produce what it's designed to produce. Kill the spirit of fear, NOW!

3. Grace

Undeserved love is a character trait that must be nurtured. The prophet Jonah forgot his place. He did not exhibit undeserved love for Nineveh. He wanted something for them (destruction), with which God wasn't in agreement. We must agree with God. We cannot allow our personal sight and emotions to interfere with the plan of God for a person or a city. First and foremost, we can never operate without grace, because we are the recipients of His AMAZING grace. It should be our privilege, delight, great joy to proclaim His will, even to those "our" flesh would ordinarily reject or be in favor of desiring destruction.

James Goll says of the prophetic intercessor, "you don't just pray to God, you learn to pray the prayers *of* God!"[28] If ***His*** heart is love, then shouldn't ours be? No matter how angry God is with us, He always has a desire for us to return, get saved, healed, and delivered.

- Inner Peace (faith related)

When the prophetic intercessor is in personal warfare, inner conflict affects the ability to see and hear clearly. When the inner eye and ear are effected or infected with

---

[28] James Goll *The Seer* by (Destiny Image Shippensburg PA 2004) 39

worldly things: worry; **man pleasing**; anxiety; **self-ambition** etc., God's agenda becomes obscured and the message of heaven muffled. Death, confusion, turmoil is then eminent. Destruction is eminent. Do you have any clue thus far that this is not good?.

- Trustworthy

Have you ever noticed that angels never botch up their assignments in scripture? They deliver the message or do the job they were sent to do, no more, no less. I am reminded of Moses and the fate he sealed for himself in Numbers 20. He had been sent with a prophetic word to an imprisoned people. His intercession had spared them time and time again. Yet, one slight slip of the spirit, which exposed a heart that had allowed pride to come in, cost him a trip ticket to enter the place where he had invested his life leading people to arrive (the Promised Land).

He broke down! Faith, patience, inner peace, grace, all weakened by the rigor of the journey. Maybe we should say this, "Can God trust you, not only to *deliver* His Word, but can He trust you to *keep* His Word?" "Can He trust you, not just with a *Word*, but with His presence, daily-" If you lose Him, you have already lost His Word. It will never find its proper place, its prayer purpose, with its proper passion. Some portion will be missing and we will have to pay the price for the lives to whom we caused failures. Our neglecting to protect His presence in us allows the enemy to have freedom to find and capture the people to whom we have been sent. How? Because our ears and eyes are the vehicle by which they are protected. If we miss God, they miss Him. If they miss Him, it may cost them their lives. We should NEVER take that lightly. One small detail missed from a strategy can cost greatly. Protect His presence.

Answer the Call

I remember when I was in college, (it seems like only a couple of years ago – ok, almost 35 yrs., but who is counting), I had an experience with God that completely terrified me. I did not understand what was going on with me. I tried to run out of my room, only to have the doors jammed shut. I fell in the floor kicking and screaming, weeping uncontrollably like a baby. Moments later, my cousin came running to that door, opened it up, because he heard me yelling "let me out, let me out." When he came in though, I wanted him to get out (ok, easy right?). Later, after I had calmed down, yet still crying and searching for answers, one of my friends said to me some even more terrifying words. He said, "I saw Carlos go through this. I believe you are being called into ministry. It's simple, just answer the call." Needless to say, it was not that simple, but 35 years later, I know more than ever, that he was "spot on" as the British say.

The call on the prophetic intercessors' life is to close the door to the demonic operations in the earth realm and open it to obedience to the Holy Spirit. Lou Engle illustrates this in a story he tells about Darlene James' (Buddhist High Priest) visit to Pasadena, California. He says,

> "The intricate sand sculpture was finished. Experienced Tibetan monks had spent hundreds of hours building it in preparation for a visit from the Dalai Lama. Accompanied by an entourage of Tibetan monks and high-level spirits he was coming to Pasadena to hold large meetings in the Civic Auditorium. Several well-known Hollywood celebrities were expected to attend. The "blessing" of the sand mandala at the Pacific Asian Museum was to be the highlight of the Dalai Lama's visit. As world leader of the Tibetan branch of Buddhism, the

Dalai Lama exerts tremendous spiritual authority. The ceremony was to create a doorway through which 722 powerful spirits could be released into the area surrounding Pasadena!

Harvest Rock Church had already experienced several significant encounters with the spirit of Buddhism. A large Buddha had once occupied center stage in the building that is now a church, placed there by the New Age cult that had occupied the campus. In 1996, with the visit of the Dali Lama approaching, we gathered the entire church together for worship and spiritual warfare. Many intercessors cried out to God in the prayer room.

We prayed for the salvation of the Dalai Lama and other Buddhists, particularly the many who are employed in Hollywood. A small group of intercessors also went down to the Pacific Asian Museum. This building, located in the center of Pasadena is right across the street from Fuller Seminary. As the group prayer-walked the museum, the anointed the perimeter of the property and laid hands on the building, sealing it all from demonic forces. At a second prayer walk, several intercessors laid a spiritual ambush at the front door, asking the Holy Spirit to touch the Dalai Lama as he walked through it.

As the day of the Dalai Lama's visit approached, a report was released that although he was going to visit the museum, he would not pray over the mandala after all! Thus Pasadena was to be spared this flood of 722 demonic spirits. Moreover, the sand from this unholy sculpture was not poured into the Arroyo Seco- the river that supplies the Los Angeles area with water-as had been planned, but was put into the sea near Santa Monica, where freak waves were reported for several days. Again, Los Angeles was spared.

A striking change of events also took place at the Civic Auditorium. Camera crews from around the world gathered on the steps of the Civic Auditorium hoping to get a few shots of the Dalai Lama with Hollywood celebrities.

Prior to this media event, an intercessor had gone to the building, laid hands on the steps, and prayed that the presence of the Lord would be released there. When the day arrived the limousine carrying the Dalai Lama pulled up to the steps. The door opened, then closed again... Then opened and closed again. This happened several times, but nobody got out of the car, spoiling this carefully planned media spectacle!

The events surrounding the Dalai Lama's visit certainly encouraged our intercessors. Although the mayor of Pasadena had given the keys of the city to the Dalai Lama, praise God the keys of the kingdom by the church's hands and if we use them, we can lock out the powers of hell!"[29]

Hearing the Voice of God

In one of the early books I have written (*The Altared Life*), I highlight the importance of listening in prayer. Often, when we pray, we spend the majority of our time talking. In a

---

[29] Lou Engle with Catherine Paine, *Digging the Wells of Revival: Reclaiming Your Historic Inheritance through Prophetic Intercession* (Shippensburg, PA: Destiny Image Publishers, 1998), 115

sense, this is a sign of our relational immaturity. In reality, the parent should do more talking than the child. It is the child who needs the wisdom of the parent. It is the child that needs instruction and direction, motivation, inspiration, in preparation for their day.

I cannot tell you how many times I have been trying to talk to my children over the years and they have been in the next room or the same room, but they missed pieces of what I was saying because a television show had captured their attention, or was too loud. Other times they were more consumed by a game they were playing, than they were with my voice.

I taught my wife and my children a unique sound that we use in stores or theatres, so we can locate each other. The sound has an obvious purpose. We never want to be lost from one another. There is a sound that we need to always know. That is the sound of the Father's voice. It is like I tell my children, "when I call your name, you should stop whatever you are doing, immediately, to answer and see what I want." That is what we should do when our Heavenly Father speaks.

6 Steps to Success

1. **Want** to Be Alone with Him
   Create space where you can spend time with God without the distractions of people, phones or personal passions. Make Him the center of your attention. Drown out the voice of every other lover.

2. **Worship** with intentional intensity for the Purpose of Intimacy
   Some people enter into worship as a religious practice. They like to do it as a part of what must be done, saying to themselves, "I know it's the right thing, to get the right result." However, intentional worship should be done not just to get something *from* God, but to be more

like God. Our worship should place us in position of such intimacy, that we experience what married people do after many years of being together and communicating. They have the uncanny ability to finish each other's statements, because they know what the other is thinking. Our intimacy with God should produce the same.

3. **Work** on Breaking Your Will (or Trading it in for His)

To operate in the realm of prophetic intercession, you must crucify your flesh. When you hear Jesus praying in the garden of Gethsemane, He is making a declaration. He is saying, "I will not operate by my will." "I am my Father's image in the earth." Hebrews 1:3 (NIV) says, "The Son is the radiance of God's glory and the exact representation of His being, sustaining all things by His powerful word. After He had provided purification for sins, He sat down at the right hand of the Majesty in heaven." Can that be said about you? "*Will* breaking" is not up to God. It is up to us. It requires a lifestyle of fasting (Read my book on Living A Lifestyle of Fasting: Breaking Through to the Best You).

Psalm 139:23, 24 is a great prayer to pray in preparation for your journey. David writes, "Search me O God, and know my heart; test me and know my anxious thoughts. See if there be any offense in me, and lead me in the way everlasting."

4. **Welcome** His Spirit as a Friend

One of the members of our church, Cherral Moore, was recently going through a time of spiritual renewal and experiencing a call to another level of ministry. She was frightened by the strong presence of God in her home because she had never experienced Him like that. She called me crying. Her husband who is very new to the spirit-filled scene, was completely withdrawn and asking her to stop. Her words to me were, "It's getting worse." When I asked her what she meant, she responded, "I cannot stop worshipping." I then responded, "It's not getting worse, it's getting better, but you may want to reword it as, "more intense." I got her to agree to that language change and moments later her attitude shifted. Finally, as she calmed down, I told her that Holy Spirit was her friend, and that she should stop fighting what she had previously given Him permission to do. I asked her to say to Him, "Welcome Holy Spirit, whatever You want of me, I will do it. Complete Your work in me. I give You permission." She did and through her experience has come a bold healing ministry.

5. **Word** Saturate Your Life

If you operate in prophetic intercession, you will often have to contend with the voice of the enemy trying to gain access to your spirit, so as to cause a, "Did God really say" moment as often as possible. The more you hear, read and say the word of God, the more confident you become that it *is* His voice you are hearing in the inner chambers of your heart. You should be able to confirm His voice by His Word. If you do not know His Word, you cannot confirm his voice. "His sheep know His Voice." (John 10:4, 5) In 1 John 4:1 (NASB) he writes "Beloved, do not believe every spirit, but test the spirits to see whether they are from God, because many false prophets have gone out into the world." When your life is saturated with the Word, you do not struggle with who is speaking to you. You know your Father's voice, by the Spirit of what is said.

6. **Write** the Vision or the "Voicing"

Prophetic intercessors are really what I call, "heavenly administrators." They are, "Spiritual Secretaries." They major in taking dictation. You should keep a pen and paper (iPad, iPhone, Tablet, Blackberry or a recorder) with you at all times so that you never miss an assignment. You should especially write down your dreams. This will require you to have a dream notebook by your bed in case you awaken in the night. Do NOT make the mistake in thinking you will go back to sleep and remember the details hours later. It's like taking notes from the teacher's lecture two hours after class or writing a movie review a week after you saw the movie. The sooner you write, the better. You also should keep a journal so you can always know what has and has not yet manifested. When you know this, you can pray... until then.

Final Thought

Lou Engle, in his book, *Digging The Wells of Revival* writes, "Human beings have intervened in the heavenly liturgy. The uninterrupted flow of consequences is dammed for a moment. New alternatives become feasible. The unexpected becomes suddenly possible, because God's people on earth have invoked heaven, the home of the possibles, and have been heard. The message is clear: History belongs to the intercessors."[30]

[30] Ibid.,115-117

Chapter 7 The Research Intercessor

Several years ago I was marveling at the number of books a very popular writer of our day had written. I was considering writing books myself and knew that it was going to require tremendous discipline and working what John Maxwell calls, "the law of trade off" in order to get it done. I was talking to a friend one day that said several things to me that helped me understand how the popular author accomplished the tall task with such a schedule. He said, "Well, it helps when you have researchers working for you." I thought to myself, "I need someone to expedite my time and pin point my aim as well." A researcher hears the subject matter and goes searching for exactly what's needed in order to build or support the topic being addressed. They come together as a comprehensive plan to expose ignorance and enhance knowledge, benefitting both the author and the reader/receiver of the completed project.

A Heart for God Notebook

I am told that Pastor Bill Winston, pastor of Living Word Christian Center in Chicago, has a member (or more) in his church who, upon hearing any vision cast from the pulpit, goes immediately to research it, bringing the found information back to him, so they can begin processing and progressing with, "God said" and not just being "hearers only." Wow! Doesn't every pastor need members like that? She may be the quintessential "Research Intercessor." Every ministry needs people all over the fellowship who keep what I call, "a heart of the pastor" notebook. Yes, you, my friend, need to get one today.

If you are an intercessor, you should never go to worship without pen and paper (or iPad, Notebook, electronic note taker), which enables you to catalog things that you need to research and to focus your time of prayer. Whether you know it or not, you are on the reconnaissance team of the Kingdom of God. Your information and intercession will be critical in keeping people alive.

Inside Information

One of my favorite stories in scripture (if you ask me next week, it may be something else...I love His Word) is the story in II Kings 6 about Elisha the prophet who could hear what the King of Syria was planning in his bedroom and then broadcast it to Israel, preparing them for every battle. Getting inside information for spiritual warfare is the job of the Research Intercessor. It is important to point out that the job of the Research Intercessor is 'the' strategic weapon of warfare intercession. Research Intercessors are the people who do spiritual mapping, which produces "intelligence on the spiritual dynamics at work in a given community...as an aid to the acquisition and interpretation of critical spiritual intelligence. Its solitary goal is to prepare the way for intercession."[31] In essence, their role is not merely to pray, it is to pray for a plan to prepare for the battle and then put together the information for the warfare intercessors.

Defining the Terms

Research is defined as "a diligent and systematic inquiry or investigation into a subject in order to discover or

---

[31] Otis, *Informed Intercession*, 114

revise facts, theories, applications, etc."[32] To search and/or search again, is its literal meaning. It really implies that one should keep digging until they have exhausted all they can find on a matter, making them an expert or at least well versed in an area.

Intercession is defined as "to go or pass between; to act between parties with a view to reconcile those who differ or contend; to interpose; to mediate." [33] An intercessor is a negotiator between two differing parties with the heart to see peace come. Elizabeth Alves, whose books on intercession are MUST buys, shares that as a warfare intercessor, she and others must know all they can about the people groups, places where they live and the policies of that area where intercession is targeted. She says, "I have recruited five research intercessors who meticulously compile and document details about the spiritual ground being covered in prayer. Research intercessors thrive on prayerfully collecting vital facts about strongholds and principalities. They help us to formulate our plan of attack." [34]

An obvious part of their assignment then is to ask God for discernment, revelation knowledge, strategies, and people to talk to with vital information that will hit the enemy's spiritual landmarks/artillery posts. Where are the strongholds in the city, community? Why do they exist? When did they start? What and who is feeding them? Are there laws, policies, and unwritten rules that affirm them? Research Intercessors find the root of the systems of evil and prepare the troops for battle there.

---

[32] http://dictionary.reference.com. Accessed: June 17, 2013.

[33] Franklin J., Ph.B.,M.A. Meine" *The Consolidated-Webster Encyclopedic Dictionary,* Consolidated Publishers (1954),384

[34] Alves, *Intercessors,* 179,180

No Cosmetic Surgery

One of the things people who watch movies and music entertainers talk about, is the changes they make over the years to maintain their appearance. Looking back at pictures from over the years is always interesting. One of my generation's greatest performers was Michael Jackson. Some would argue that he was one of the best of all time. Nevertheless, the point is this, watching Michael as I did growing up, was very interesting. His childhood performances that I saw when they would come over from Gary, Indiana to Chicago, were spectacular. Everyone loved the "Jackson 5". As the years went on, Michael developed into a music icon. He went through changes with his weight, the color of his skin, and an obvious cosmetic surgery to his nose. He was trying to do all he could to appeal to his adoring fan base. At the same time, not enough people were paying attention to the apparently not so obvious demonic challenges he was facing that were becoming a stronghold in his life. The cosmetic surgery was insufficient in the end, to save his life. There were some root problems that needed serious research and strategic intercession in order to deliver him from an undetectable ugliness. Research Intercessors NEVER settle for cosmetic surgery. It is not even a consideration. Medicine to address the symptoms and nothing to destroy the root, is not an option.

God Goggles

One of the examples of Research Intercessors in the Bible is found in the book of Numbers. In Numbers 13:1-2, 17-20(NASB), Moses sends 12 spies on a recon assignment as directed by God:
"¹Then the LORD spoke to Moses saying, ² "Send out for yourself men so that they may spy out the land of Canaan, which I am going to give to the sons of Israel; you shall send a man from each of their fathers' tribes, every one a leader

among them...¹⁷ When Moses sent them to spy out the land of Canaan, he said to them, "Go up there into the Negev; then go up into the hill country. ¹⁸ See what the land is like, and whether the people who live in it are strong or weak, whether they are few or many. ¹⁹ How is the land in which they live, is it good or bad? And how are the cities in which they live, are they like open camps or with fortifications? ²⁰ How is the land, is it fat or lean? Are there trees in it or not? Make an effort then to get some of the fruit of the land." Now the time was the time of the first ripe grapes."

They followed his directions, found the information, but the report they brought back was one that caused fear, not faith to fight, in the hearts of the people. Listen to their research report in Numbers 13: 25-33 (NASB):

> "²⁵ When they returned from spying out the land, at the end of forty days, ²⁶ they proceeded to come to Moses and Aaron and to all the congregation of the sons of Israel in the wilderness of Paran, at Kadesh; and they brought back word to them and to all the congregation and showed them the fruit of the land. ²⁷ Thus they told him, and said, "We went in to the land where you sent us; and it certainly does flow with milk and honey, and this is its fruit. ²⁸ Nevertheless, the people who live in the land are strong, and the cities are fortified and very large; and moreover, we saw the descendants of Anak there. ²⁹ Amalek is living in the land of the Negev and the Hittites and the Jebusites and the Amorites are living in the hill country, and the Canaanites are living by the sea and by the side of the Jordan." ³⁰ Then Caleb quieted the people before Moses and said, "We should by all means go up and take possession of it, for we will surely overcome it. ³¹ But the men who had gone up with him said, "We are

not able to go up against the people, for they are too strong for us." ³² So they gave out to the sons of Israel a bad report of the land which they had spied out, saying, "The land through which we have gone, in spying it out, is a land that devours its inhabitants; and all the people whom we saw in it are men of great size. ³³ There also we saw the Nephilim (the sons of Anak are part of the Nephilim); and we became like grasshoppers in our own sight, and so we were in their sight."

Their report came back from ten of the twelve, that this is not a war worth fighting. However, the warfare was not optional. God sent them there to seize the land. The ten only gave the report they did, because they were not wearing God Goggles. It is the job of the Research Intercessors to see what God sees, not what their flesh sees. What looks impossible from the eyes of the flesh is not impossible with God. The Research Intercessor must wipe out every flesh issue so that they see clearly. Satan is a flesh eater. He knew the children of Israel had a history of fear and rebellion and he exposes it one more time, as one more effort to delay their destiny (or better yet, prevent it). Put your God Goggles on and keep them on!

Background Check

We often do extensive background checks of persons working in our daycares or working with our youth. It is important to know who they are before they begin so we ward off any abuse problems. Companies also do background checks for employers before they are hired. One of the things they do is check references. I have received countless calls over the years from employers asking about the character traits of people who put me down as a reference (some of which shouldn't have). That said, let me ask you a question. If we really believe that we are at war (spiritually), and we know the enemy is strong and deceptive, why would we just send anyone in to do reconnaissance work? Shouldn't we make sure that the people who do this very important, strategic work are ready in every way? I want to offer several qualities to consider that Research Intercessors must have. This list is not exhaustive. However, it will help you as you think about whether you or people who claim to work in this area of intercession are qualified.

Research Intercessor Qualifications

I. You Must Love God and See What He Sees

    A. Loving God begins with what He wants for you and others

    B. Loving God means you have a Word and prayer-centered life

    C. Loving God means you wake up with a desire to serve daily

    D. Loving God means everything you do has 'glorifying God' written all over it

II. You Must Have a Love for People (Good and Bad)

    A. Loving people means you must desire souls to be saved and people to be delivered from bondage

    B. Loving people means you must see every person as a harvest. When Jesus looked at the people in Matt. 9:35-38 (NASB), He felt compassion. "[35] Jesus was going through all the cities and villages, teaching in their synagogues and proclaiming the gospel of the kingdom, and healing every kind of disease and every kind of sickness. ³⁶ Seeing the people, He felt compassion for them, because they were distressed and dispirited like sheep without a shepherd. ³⁷ *Then* He said to His disciples, "The harvest is plentiful, but the workers are few. ³⁸ Therefore beseech the Lord of the harvest to send out workers into His harvest."

C. Loving people means you must say to yourself, "These are my brothers and my sisters; and I'm not going to see them bound. I have the key to their freedom. I will not walk away silent." Isaiah 62:1-4 (NASB) states, "For Zion's sake I will not keep silent, And for Jerusalem's sake I will not keep quiet, Until her righteousness goes forth like brightness, And her salvation like a torch that is burning. ² The nations will see your righteousness, And all kings your glory; And you will be called by a new name Which the mouth of the LORD will designate. ³ You will also be a crown of beauty in the hand of the LORD, And a royal diadem in the hand of your God.
⁴ It will no longer be said to you, "Forsaken," Nor to your land will it any longer be said, "Desolate"; But you will be called, "My delight is in her," And your land, "Married"; For the LORD delights in you, And to Him your land will be married."

III. You Must Not Be Lazy

A. Not being lazy means that you must have a commitment to work. It takes time and energy to do this assignment.

  B. Not being lazy means that *surface* information will not satisfy when the *deep* is waiting

  C. Not being lazy means that being there is not enough. Making an impact that causes a crisis in hell, is always our primary goal.

IV. You Must Love History

  A. Loving history means that much of the work is about *uncovering* history. Sometimes that history goes way back.

  B. Loving history means that you don't forget that it is not a 'history only' seeking event; but history for the purposes of breaking chains.

  C. Loving history means that it's always about replacing unfruitful history for HIS-story in that place.

V. You Must Enjoy Reading

  A. Enjoying reading means that you remember you can't research without reading

  B. Enjoying reading means that you use books, magazines, websites, newspapers, (current and old), and any other tools necessary

  C. Need I say more?

VI. You Need Administrative Skills

    A. Organized – time, meetings, balanced so that family and personal development don't go lacking

    B. Organization – people around you that keep you focused as well and that you report to

    C. Ordered - in all you do so that when you pass your work off others can take it and run to the finish line

    D. A spirit of excellence is needed because this is for HIM. Kingdom things should be done on earth as they are in Heaven.

VII. You Must Be Finishers

    A. Being a finisher means that every moment you delay getting your work done is a day that the warriors are delayed in their attack and the enemy is advancing

    B. Being a finisher means that seeing the end in mind is only the beginning. You must have a mind to see it end (with your hands)

Primary Purpose of Research
(Refer Back to the Chapter on Taking Your City)

George Otis gives us six categories for Research Intercessors to look into as they begin the process of reaching God's expected end in their territory.

1. The status of Christianity (which directs us to the question about what's wrong with this community?)

2. What are the prevailing social bondages (which directs us to the same question, what's wrong with the community)?

3. What are the world views and allegiances (which again directs us to the same question about community)?

4. What are the spiritual oppositions (which directs us to the same question)?

5. What has been the evolution of the current circumstance (which raises the question concerning where the problem came from)?

6. What is the potential for significant breakthroughs (which raises the question of what can be done to change what we have discovered)? This is the end desire of All research.

People Are Our Business

Otis says, "God is not doing our work for us. He is pointing us in the right direction. The appropriate response is to thank Him for the tip and then roll up our sleeves."[35] Research Intercessors, unlike many other intercessors, MUST be "people persons." Talking to, and walking with people, are a part of the package. While other intercessors (at least it may seem) find themselves in the comfort of their homes and churches, there are times the Research Intercessor must do interviews, prayer walks, and attend community events. When you are called to this area of intercession, you must deal with the *demons* of Your and others, ANCESTRY. Every bit of anger, pride, racism, discrimination, etc. needs to have come under subjection to the will of God. You may be called to meet with the very ancestry of the people who you were taught to despise,

---

[35] Otis, *Informed Intercession*, 174

distrust, or even hate. If any flesh remains, the enemy will prevent you from gaining necessary information, after God has opened a door for you to get it, because instead of seeing what He sees in the future, you are looking backwards. (e.g. Book of Jonah regarding Ninevah)

Final Thoughts

If you are ego-driven, you won't survive here. Really you will not survive anywhere, but in the world's system. There, Satan will promise to take good care of you (and that my dear friend is a deception). Deception *is* his DNA anyway. As I began this chapter, I talked about the story of a very popular author who put out many books. I mentioned that it is projected that researchers were the key to that happening. I did not mention, however, that none of their pictures or names are on the outside cover of any of his books. They have not been asked to go and do any speaking tours or book signing tours. Although they are privately recognized, there is no public fanfare; yet not one book would have been published nor one person blessed had not they been involved. Never forget that, and know that your reward is coming. God will honor your work. Warning, warning...."DO NOT EVER," do this work unto men, or for the compliments of others. If your fulfillment is tied to them, your output will be up and down. You will work for applause from the wrong fan base (the worlds) and boos will cause you distraction and to be dysfunctional. Stay tuned only to heaven. Know your worth. The cheers of heaven never cease for you. You are a critical part of our army that we cannot do without. Get busy and stay busy, we need you more than you know. As a matter of fact I hear heaven calling your name now and I am standing proudly cheering with them.

Chapter 8 The Warfare Intercessor

Many years ago, the popular singing group, The Temptations, recorded a controversial song entitled "War." It was a song that spoke in opposition to the war in Vietnam. Two years later, the song was recorded again and made popular, rising to number one on the pop charts, by a solo artist by the name of Edwin Starr.[36] The Norman Whitfield-written song's opening lyrics are "War, huh! What is it good for? Absolutely nothing." [37] The song goes on to describe all the ills of war, from tears to fears, to heartbreaks. It speaks of wars' destructive power. Whitfield had a point.

War does have a destructive power. But, war can also be constructive in the fact that it can be used to free people. It still destroys, but all destruction is not bad. Some destruction is necessary for peace to prevail. Without the intercession of other nations in World War II, Germany would have annihilated the Jewish people. As a matter of fact, the reason for intercession when others are under attack, is because not to get involved, is eventually to invite the warmonger to our doorstep as well. Hitler needed to know that he was not fighting a helpless, hopeless people. His hatred sparked a rise of intercession from around the world. The war was on!

---

[36] http://en.wikipedia.org/wiki/War_(Edwin_Starr_song). Accessed June 17,2013

[37] http://lyrics.wikia.com/Edwin_Starr:War, Accessed June 17,2013

They're Fighting Over Me

Elizabeth Alves says, "All spiritual warfare is a fight over one thing: Truth."[38] So if Jesus said that *He* is the Truth, then is the *warfare* over Him? Well, sort of! It *is* over Him, but it is over the Him, in Us. We are *His* body in the earth, for the purpose of being fruitful, multiplying replenishing the earth and having dominion. This is a battle over dominion. Is God truth, or a lie? Satan is still questioning man in this regard. "Did God really say…"[39], is his question for the ages. This whole warfare is about restoration of rights, purity of purpose, "image" consulting. Jeremiah 29:11 (NASB) says,

> [11] 'For I know the plans that I have for you,' declares the LORD, 'plans for welfare and not for calamity to give you a future and a hope.'

He says, "I would like you to receive what you lost in Eden" The bottom line is, this fight is over you and me. We represent the best of all God created.

Defining the Terms

The Random House Dictionary defines war as "a major armed conflict as between nations; any struggle or fight; the science of military operations; to be in a state of strong opposition."[40]

Intercession is defined as "to go or pass between; to act between parties with a view to reconcile those who differ or contend; to interpose; to mediate."[41] Dutch Sheets says, "Intercession, according to our definition involves two very different activities. One is reconciling, the other is separating.

---

[38] Alves, *Intercession*, 143

[39] Genesis 3:1 (NIV)

[40] Random House Dictionary, Ballentine Books, NY:NY., 1980 998

[41] Alves, Intercessors, 38

One is a tearing away – a disuniting, the other a joining to – a uniting. This is what Christ did through His work of intercession, and it's what we do in our continuation of it. In light of this, it is important to realize that much of our intercession must be a combination of the two. It is often not enough to simply ask the Father to do something, although this is most Christians' total concept of prayer. Many think it is necessary to accompany asking, with a spiritual warfare or wrestling, enforcing a victory of Calvary."[42]

Dutch Sheets cites, and I agree, that it is virtually impossible to talk about intercession and not include war. To intercede for anyone or anything is actually to be at war with the enemy for that person's faith. You are standing in position to defend, with your life, what you are praying about. You are asking God's backing as well.

The War Within

When Jesus was in the Garden of Gethsemane, praying for direction regarding the cross, He was in warfare. Souls were weighing in the balance (mine and yours too). The Bible says that the battle was so intense that He perspired drops of blood. He was really warring with His life internally.

> Paul says in Romans 7:18:23 (NASB):
> [18] For I know that nothing good dwells in me, that is, in my flesh; for the willing is present in me, but the doing of the good is not. [19] For the good that I want, I do not do, but I practice the very evil that I do not want. [20] But if I am doing the very thing I do not want, I am no longer the one doing it, but sin which dwells in me. [21] I find then the principle that evil is present in me,

---

[42] Sheets, *Intercessory Prayer*, 136

the one who wants to do good. ²² For I joyfully concur with the law of God in the inner man, ²³ but I see a different law in the members of my body, waging war against the law of my mind and making me a prisoner of the law of sin which is in my members."

He also writes in Ephesians 6:12 (NASB):
"[12] For our struggle is not against flesh and blood, but against the rulers, against the powers, against the world forces of this darkness, against the spiritual forces of wickedness in the heavenly places."

This warfare is not something we take lightly. It is an internal job that seeks to destroy us and is orchestrated in the spirit realm. Jesus experienced warfare in Matthew 4 and in Luke 4 which, in a way, gives us a clear indication that we will not be exempt from the same. Satan is after the Christ in us. He will challenge us to find some weakness, some open wound, some place of pride, anywhere there is an opening that will expose why it is not to our advantage, nor to the worlds, to follow God. He has an idea of your potential and desires to allow you freedom to roam with your spiritual idiosyncrasies, so that he can expose them at the most opportune time. That time we know, arises from the enemy where he sees an opportunity to expose us, which will give him the greatest joy, God the greatest pain and you the greatest embarrassment.

The War Without

We are constantly concentrating on wars between our nations of the world, because prideful men cannot handle power, believing that their form of governing is undeniably the model for all to follow. At the root of these wars may seem to be merely philosophical differences in the minds of men, but is really a spiritual defect. Wars have always been a way of straightening out what men have disagreed on, as well as what God has opposed. It has been standard operating procedure since the fall of man. However, we do not place enough emphasis on the spiritual undercover or undertones of the wars between men. Notice, I keep calling them, "wars between men." They are just that! They are decided by men; often by one man against another. When men are family-oriented and mature, they make decisions like Abraham did with Lot. Abraham decided that, because their men could not get along, it was appropriate not to war but to part in peace. This is the ideal. But, in reality, egos prevail and incite warfare.

The ego of Satan is always at work. Therefore, while the earth remains, there will be warfare and spoils. WE are going to be at war. So decide *where* you stand, and then, STAND. Know this, in the end, we win! I just thought you needed to hear that, so you can have a thought to remember when times get tough. That thought will encourage you to take a quick praise break on your way to, or in the midst of, a battle.

C. Peter Wagner, in his book *Warfare Prayer*, cites three levels of spiritual warfare:

> Ground-level: The ministry of casting out demons primarily in people
>
> Occult-level: The ministry of dealing with the people who promote demonic activity as well as organizations that are disguised as Godly and spiritual but not spirit-filled
>
> Strategic-level: The ministry of territorial spirits being cast out

Each of these warfare levels deals with the demonic, but each goes higher and higher. Wagner intimates that at first glance all of these appear to be the same. But, at closer inspection, you can see the difference.

Commenting on the final of the three areas, he writes, "A clear biblical occurrence of strategic-level warfare is found in Revelation 12 where we are told, "war broke out in heaven. Michael and his angels fought against the dragon; and the dragon and his angels fought (Rev. 12:7). This is something quite different from dealing with the occult or casting out demons of lust."[43]

Did God Really Say...

Genesis 3 tells the story of the fall. Two chapters in the Bible define or describe our beginning. One chapter describes our fall from dominion, grace, perfection, image reflection. The rest of biblical history is a story about vision, redemption and the warfare that ensues because of the great love God has for us, verses the will Satan has to sabotage it. Genesis 3 raises the eternal question (as we mentioned a bit earlier), that promotes doubt in the mind of every believer. "Did God really say?" is what the serpent asks of Eve and us.

There are some serious issues being debated in our time. They challenge the very fiber/foundation of our being/existence. They are moral debates. We have mistakenly labeled them right wing verses left wing, or Republican verses Democratic issues. They are the serpent questions of our day.

Are you sure God meant that only Adam and Eve could constitute a marriage?

Don't you think God meant that women should choose whether they should bring a baby to term or not (abortion)?

---

[43] C. Peter Wagner, *Warfare Prayer*, Revised edition ed. (Ventura, CA: Regal Books, 1997), 19

Are you sure God doesn't want us to obey the law of the land? (Government rule)

The warfare today is for the family. The very first institution established in scripture for the purpose of populating the earth and maintaining dominion. If you destroy a foundation, you eventually watch a building fall. Families are no different. They are the building cornerstone of society. The warfare for life, family, and the right government are at the top of the list in this generation (and every one hereafter). We must war on behalf of our kingdom's government being established, because it always promotes life and family. It promotes life in the womb, and supports life outside of the womb.

II Corinthians 10:4 (NASB) says:
"for the weapons of our warfare are not of the flesh, but divinely powerful for the destruction of fortresses."

Beyond a shadow of a doubt, arguments of the enemy must be cast down. This is no place for "wimps." Taking captive anything that the enemy has is a task for "superman." You are that person. Holy-spirit filled, fire-baptized (flesh burned away) people, are "special forces, super heroes" that the devil hates to see coming.

Where crime, gangs, poverty, abortion, racism, classicism, greed, sexual abuse, drugs, prostitution, embraced homosexuality, divorce, child abuse, spousal abuse, spiritual abuse, etc. is found in our cities, I agree with Peter Wagner, it reflects temporary victory for Satan. We do need all the programs we can, to start to help combat these ills. We need to do all the demonstrations, marches, town meetings, city hall sit-ins, legislation, call-ins we can, however, we need to understand, that the real battle is a spiritual one.

When Warfare and Intercession Meet

One of my spiritual daughters was telling me about a movie involving a gang in the New York area. One scene found a rival gang calling out their enemy by saying, "Warriors, come out and play." [44] As soon as I heard that, it was like a light went on. Then it became a clarion call as I began to say, "Warriors, come out and Pray!" That's my cry to this generation. Warriors of God, it's time to come out and pray.

Elizabeth Alves writes, "Sin, unforgiveness and rebellion render us impotent, and prove that we are living independently of God (See I Samuel 5:22, Isaiah 59:2). Sin causes people to come under Satan's authority and binds them from being free to obey God (see Rom. 8:7). Therefore, warfare intercessors are those who fight to reestablish God's authority in places where people have lost their freedom to choose dependence upon Him."[45] While I fully agree that this is the motivational and foundational cause for warfare intercession, it has another side to it. Warfare intercession arises to fight to free those under the bondage of sin for certain. It also rises, as in the case of Exodus 17 and II Chronicles 20, to *protect* the people of God against their oppressors or enemies.

In Joshua 7, after the defeat of the only war recorded in Joshua's tenure, he cries out to God along with his elders/leaders. He seeks understanding for why a battle has been lost, and God answers strangely. He tells Joshua that the enemy has infiltrated Israel in the person of a fellow brother (Achan). This is another kind of warfare! And yet, it is an integral part that the warfare intercessor must learn. What to do with losses and internal issues is critical to warfare prayer. We must constantly ask questions in intercession. "Why are we suffering loss?" "Is there enemy within?" "Is there something

---

[44]http://en.wikiquote.org/wiki/The_Warriors, Accessed June 17,2013

[45]Alves, Intercessors, 147

we have done to offend our Father, His Son, or Holy Spirit?" "Are we under friendly fire (which is really not friendly at all)?" These are all post-battle questions that must be raised before God, for the purpose of evaluating casualties. These questions were the key to returning to battle and winning the war against the same enemy that had defeated Joshua and Gods' army. There, beloved *should* be an oxymoron, defeated God's army. Those words should never be together (defeated army of God).

Genesis 18 records a classic story of warfare intercession. Abraham, knowing that his nephew and family are in Sodom, battles for the salvation of the city in passionate prayer before God. This story is an example of how intercessory prayer overlaps in many areas. This story could be shared as one of "Family Intercession" as well. Yet, it undoubtedly qualifies under the category of warfare. All of the characteristics of the statement of Elizabeth Alves are there concerning why warfare prayer is instituted: sin, rebellion and living independently of God. A whole region had come to a place where they were under the influence of Satan. Here is the question for you my friend, "Is your city under siege?" Well, are you warring for their freedom? Abraham is fighting for his family, yes; but, notice his word usage.

"Will You indeed sweep away the righteous with the wicked?" (Gen. 18:23 NASB)

Then he goes back and forth with God beginning with asking if He (God) located 50, would that be enough to save the city, and he keeps repeating the request until he gets to 10, "*righteous*" people.

The Battle for Us

Early in the ministry of Jesus, He teaches the disciples to pray. One of the initial lines in the "Model Prayer" is "Thy kingdom come, thy will be done…" [46] Jesus would come face to face with that very prayer in the Garden of Gethsemane. He is at war. His earth suit (flesh) battles for a say so in the matter of how salvation would come to the world. Luke 22:44 says that the battle became so intense within, that blood was coming forth from His body.

There is also a fight within us. We too experience a war within us to determine whether our words in the earth are genuine before God, or mere shiny trophies to be paraded by men for our names to be found in their mental hall of fame. Who are you here for?

Cindy Jacobs says, "In the battle of Gethsemane Jesus intentionally went to fight a war in the heavenlies to make a way for His triumph at Calvary. Can you imagine what the battleground in the heavenlies looked while Jesus travailed in the Garden? The angels of God blazing forth, preparing for the greatest war for the souls of humankind ever fought."[47] He went to war for US! He battled internally, externally (with men) and in the spiritual realm ("...spiritual forces of wickedness in the heavenly places" Eph. 6:12 NASB). He settled everything to give us our rights back as the fruitful, multipliers, replenishers, dominion carriers that we were created to be in (Genesis 1: 27-28)! You should've taken a praise break right there! Ok, that said, if you are going to be in, or are called into, warfare intercession, then Give it Your All. Don't wait for battles to come to you. "Set your face towards today's Jerusalem and go fight/War, on behalf of this generation (Luke 9:51).

Choose Your Weapons

[46] Matthew 6:10 KJV

[47] Jacobs, *Possessing The Gates of The Enemy*, 55

In any war, weapons are essential instruments for victorious outcome. In biblical times the sword, shield, daggers, and spears were used. Javelins were thrown, slings used, stones hurled, and bows and arrows propelled in many wars/battles. However, they were not the only weapons used. There were times God suggested unconventional weapons for the people in order to do two things: (1) demonstrate His power and: (2) gain an understanding of the level of their faith. In Joshua 6 he uses a shout. In II Chronicles 20, He uses praise and worship. In II Kings 6, Elisha uses the weapon of faith.

II Corinthians 10:3-4, which we have already mentioned, there is used the word "carnal", when describing the weapons we do ***not*** use. That word carnal comes from the Greek word sarkikós (pronounced sar-kee-kos') which means "pertaining to flesh, bodily, temporal." [48] In other words, they are man-made instruments. Our weapons cannot be controlled by men. Therefore, when they are used, men cannot take credit for them.

C. Peter Wagner writes, "We are so used to trying to solve social and economic problems through politics, or legal problems through the courts, or personal disagreements, through arguing about them, or international relationships through war, that to hear that God has a higher and more effective way through spiritual weapons is regarded as wishful thinking, even by many born-again Christians. This attitude needs to change."13 Without a doubt I agree. If God can win once with weapons of faith, praise, worship, a shout, prayer, then He can do it again. By the way, all of these weapons were used in the Old Testament. I believe and know from experience, that they are still good today.

In the New Testament, new weapons were added to our arsenal as well: The Name of Jesus, The Blood of Jesus,

---

[48] W.E. Vine, *Vine's Complete Expository Dictionary of Old and New Testament Words: with Topical Index* (Nashville: Thomas Nelson, 1996), 89

Agreement, and "It is Written." We have enough to defeat any foe. Our victory lies within us. Who wins? A God said? Or a, did God really say?

The Name of Jesus: No Greater Name

When I was in the eighth grade, I attended a school which was outside of our district. Although the school was filled with excellent teachers, the Chicago inner-city was in the middle of a huge gang recruitment. The school I attended, and the neighborhood I lived in, had two different gangs running them. Because I was involved in sports, I pretty much did not have to worry about being hassled as long as I didn't cross any boundaries. On the corner of our school was a little store that sold great hamburgers, but was off limits to "civilians," or non-gang members. For some reason (a hamburger and some candy I am sure), I really wanted to go in there. One day, I was talking to one of my former schoolmates from kindergarten through sixth grade. Her brother came outside and began to talk to me. He asked me where I was going to school and I told him. He then said to me, "If anyone gives you any trouble, tell them Monk Brown is your cousin." At that time, he was big, as a name on the gang scene. So when I went back to school, I went right into that corner store. They asked me what I was doing in there. I simply told them what I was doing and then did the "name drop" thing. Everybody paused. Someone asked, "Monk Brown is your cousin?" I said, "Yes." They then said, "Pass," which meant I was free to have access to the property. I, in other words, could get into where I had been denied, and then could ask for whatever I wanted.

Philippians 2:9 (NASB) says,

"For this reason also, God highly exalted Him, and bestowed on Him the name which is above every name,"

He said that every person would eventually have to bow and submit to the authority of that name. John 14:14 (NASB) records Jesus saying:

"If you ask Me anything in My name, I will do it."

When the 120 came back from their fact find, disciple discovery mission, they returned with a revelation. Luke 10:17 indicates that they anxiously, surprisingly tell Jesus that even the demons responded to His name in submission. That name, Jesus, has power in it and should be used only by permission to those who have been given authority to do so.

The Blood of Jesus

There are several passages of scripture that refer to the power of the blood. Then there are others that specifically point to the blood of Jesus. Read the following:

I. About the Power of the Blood

    A.   Leviticus 17:11, 14 (NASB) [11] For the life of the flesh is in the blood, and I have given it to you on the altar to make atonement for your souls; for it is the blood by reason of the life that makes atonement.'
[14] "For as for the life of all flesh, its blood is identified with its life. Therefore I said to the sons of Israel, 'You are not to eat the blood of any flesh, for the life of all flesh is its blood; whoever eats it shall be cut off.'

    B.   Exodus 12:13 (NASB) *[13] The blood shall be a sign for you on the houses where you live; and when I see the blood I will pass over you, and no plague will befall you to destroy you when I strike the land of*

Egypt.

C.	Exodus 29:37 (NASB) *³⁷ For seven days you shall make atonement for the altar and consecrate it; then the altar shall be most holy, and whatever touches the altar shall be holy.*

II.	About Jesus' Specifically

A.	Hebrews 9:14 (NASB) how much more will the blood of Christ, who through the eternal Spirit offered Himself without blemish to God, cleanse your conscience from dead works to serve the living God?

B.	Hebrews 9:22 (NASB) And according to the Law, one may almost say, all things are cleansed with blood, and without shedding of blood there is no forgiveness

C.	Hebrews 10:19,22 (NASB) ¹⁹ Therefore, brethren, since we have confidence to enter the holy place by the blood of Jesus,… ²² let us draw near with a sincere heart in full assurance of faith, having our hearts sprinkled clean from an evil conscience and our bodies washed with pure water.

D.	Hebrews 13:22 (NASB) But I urge you, brethren, bear with this word of exhortation, for I have written to you briefly.

E.	I John 1:7 (NASB) but if we walk in the Light as He Himself is in the Light, we have fellowship with one another, and the blood of Jesus His Son cleanses us from all sin.

F.   Revelation 1:5 (NASB) and from Jesus Christ, the faithful witness, the firstborn of the dead, and the ruler of the kings of the earth. To Him who loves us and released us from our sins by His blood"

All of these are powerful scriptures that indicate the power of the blood of Jesus. However, one in particular and specifically speaks to its ability in the warfare realm.
Rev. 12:11 says this,

"And they overcame him (Satan, the accuser of the brethren) because of the blood of the lamb and because of the word of their testimony…!"

The archangel, Michael, wins the great warfare with the dragon because he has at his disposal the blood of the Lamb, Jesus, and so do we.

Agreement: "That They May Be One"

When Jesus prays in John 17, he did not pray exactly according to the prayer he taught the disciples in Matthew 6/Luke 11. He is preparing for His departure and He knows that He needs the disciples to use their oneness as a strength. He prays and asks the Father to show them how to be one even as He and the Father are one. In Acts 2 it is evident that the baptism of the Holy Spirit does not come merely based on them being in one place, but being on one accord. Many churches have the one place down pat, but are far apart in heart and purpose. It is the one accord that brings forth the power to change atmospheres.

Matthew 18:19 (NASB) says,

"Again I say to you, that if two of you agree on earth about anything that they may ask, it shall be done for them by My Father who is in heaven.

Amos 3:3 (NASB) says, ³ Do two men walk together unless they have made an appointment?

In Genesis 11, heaven was affected by the oneness of a wayward people which caused the scattering of languages so that they would not be able to do anything too crazy. Listen to the story:

> ¹¹ Now the whole earth used the same language and the same words. ² It came about as they journeyed east, that they found a plain in the land of Shinar and settled there. ³ They said to one another, "Come, let us make bricks and burn them thoroughly." And they used brick for stone, and they used tar for mortar. ⁴ They said, "Come, let us build for ourselves a city, and a tower whose top will reach into heaven, and let us make for ourselves a name, otherwise we will be scattered abroad over the face of the whole earth." ⁵ The LORD came down to see the city and the tower which the sons of men had built. ⁶ The LORD said, "Behold, they are one people, and they all have the same language. And this is what they began to do, and now nothing which they purpose to do will be impossible for them."

It is Written: The Authority of His Word

Every time the devil came to Jesus in Matthew 4, He responded, "It is Written." Every time He did, the conversation shifted to another test until the devil had enough. Notice, however, that Jesus had come directly out of a fast. It is important to note that warfare intercessors need to have "a fasted life." If you go to battle with ANY flesh issues, you will be eaten alive until you have lost your confidence.

Jesus could not say anything but, "it is written," because when you are fasting properly you are eating a healthy portion of Word at every meal. You are sacrificing, along with praying, over those replacement meals. So, in other words, whatever you put in, will come back out when under pressure. And make no mistake about it, warfare *is* pressure.

Let's Get Ready to Rumble

Michael Buffer, the famed sports announcer always set us up for the big main event fights with the introduction, "Let's Get Ready to R-R-R-Rumble!" That was always exciting. Everyone knew that the fight was soon coming. Anticipation was high and the fans were buzzing with excitement. The fighters would be going through their last minute check offs and warming up, staying loose. All the training came down to this one moment. It is "put up or shut up time." This is where it is all put on the line. At this point, you (the fighter) are not thinking about what you should have done differently to prepare or how that will affect you in the fight. It boils down to one thing, "What do I have to do to win?"

This is Not a Boxing Match

Although we often find ourselves in shadow boxing matches with the enemy, this is not a sport. It is a war; and, it is for all the "marbles." Life is on the line. Just like fighters prepare for a fight by training, so must we in the area of spiritual warfare. There are six principles, or laws, I want to list that need to be kept near to the head and heart:

1. The Law of Harvest – You will get back from your efforts what you put into it

2. The Law of Hard Work – Do not ever give less than your absolute best. Hear God and do your part. It will pay off, even if you cannot see it.

3. The Law of Humility – You plant your prayers, research and work. Paul writes, "but God gives the increase." Know that He uses you and be grateful.

4. The Law of Holding Back – Be selfless in battle. Don't let fear get involved. Fight all out as though lives depend upon it, because they do. PRAY HARD. Don't look back in the regret, that had you pressed in, something better could have been.

5. The Law of Heating Up – Do not let the enemy get you frustrated.

6. The Law of Healing – Take time to reflect, recover, evaluate so that you can be strong every time you go to battle.

Know Your Opponent: Prepare for War

Kay Arthur asks us, "How accurate and complete is your information on your enemy, the devil?"[49] General Matthew B. Ridgeway in his autobiography, *Soldier*, wrote, "There are two kinds of information that no commander can do without – information pertaining to the enemy which we call 'combat intelligence' and information on the terrain. Both are

---

[49] Kay Arthur, *Lord, Is It Warfare? Teach Me to Stand: a Devotional Study On Spiritual Victory*, 1st WaterBrook Press ed. (Colorado Springs, Colo.: WaterBrook Press, 2000), 31

vital. Accurate, and up-to-date, intelligence on the enemy is crucial in making tactical decisions in war. A thorough knowledge of the strength of your opposition, the enemy's probable line of attack, and the enemy's tactics all help determine the course a nation's land sea, and air divisions will take."[50]

Everything the bible says about the devil should be known by Warfare Intercessors; beginning in Genesis 3 to the book of Revelations. Here are a few of the scriptures you need to study:

Gen. 3:1-24	Ezekiel 28:11-19
Isaiah 14:3-15	Job 1:1-22; 2:1-10
Matt. 4/ Luke 4	Matt. 13:24-30; 28, 39
Luke 13:26; 22:31	Acts 10:38
John 10:10	II Cor. 4:4
Eph. 2:1-3	I Tim. 3:6
II Tim. 3:1-8	James 4:7-8
I Peter 5:6-11	III John 1:9-11
Rev. 9	Rev. 12:3-11

Learn his names, so you recognize his spirit anywhere. Do not ever forget who you are fighting. He does not fight fair and he will kill you if you put your guard down. We are depending on you mighty warrior. Don't let us down. Go study all you can in this area. There are many books on this subject area. Authors and Warfare Intercessors that you can Google:

C. Peter Wagner	*Territorial Spirits*
Cindy Jacobs	*Possessing the Gates of The Enemy*
Kay Arthur	*Lord, Is it War?*
Paul and Clair Hollis	*This Means War*
Dr. Daniel Olukoya	Warfare Intercessor

---

[50] Ibid.,32

Dr. Cindy Trimm   Warfare Intercessor
Elizabeth Alves   *Becoming a Prayer Warrior*

Chapter 9 The Bridal Intercessor

One of the most exciting times in life (especially for most brides) is the planning of their wedding. Have you ever looked into the eyes of a truly happy bride-to-be? While there may be nervous tension, apprehension, yet cool, calm, collective verbiage falling from the lips of the groom, the bride is rarely (if ever) that way. She is gaining her "knight in shining armor." She is preparing to be given away to the man of her dreams. She is anticipating the birth of children and a life of love that will last until eternity meets them.

The uniting of true love is indeed a beautiful thing. I should know, I see it as a reflection, whenever I look into my wife's eyes. Why should she have all the excitement? I mean, it was my wedding too!

In the book of Revelation we are given the same picture, "Let us rejoice and be glad and give the glory to Him, for the marriage of the Lamb has come and His bride has made herself ready. It was given to her to clothe herself in fine linen, bright and clean; for the fine linen is the righteous acts of the saints."(Revelation 19:7, 8 NASB)

The picture of rejoicing comes about as a result of both parties preparing for this anticipated arrival date. The marriage has come. That my dear friend, is going to be *some* kind of day.

The Two Faces Of Bridal Intercession
(Two Schools Of Thought)

There are really only two sources (that I could find) out today in this quiet but powerful area. So, as I write, this is an area of growth for the body of Christ. In a sense, it covers all areas of intercession, and yet, one of the two sources makes this area a "specialists" group. I will address that area first, because I see a revelation in it and a biblical precedent being set, of which we would do well to take note.

Single and Satisfied

In a sense, the model for one form of bridal intercession is found in the Catholic Church. The priesthood and nunnery both take what is called as, "A Vow of Chastity". That vow calls for them to stay single, not marry, have no earthly companion to call spouse and procreate. This vow is in essence a vow to make oneself readily available to any desire that the bridegroom (Jesus), has for their life. Dr. Pernell Hewing, founder of a powerful ministry called "The Sanctuary" in Whitewater Wisconsin, and writer of multiple books on prayer, writes, "Have you been waiting for that mate, wanting so much for that special person to come home with so you can share your life? Give up the search and center your love on the bridegroom." [51] Dr. Hewing believes, and I concur, that this is a special call upon the life of the individual. When a person answers this call, it is as serious as any commitment to holy matrimony. Some people (male *or* female) may not be suited for earthly matrimony, even though they are without a doubt meant for intimacy.

In the case of Mary (mother of Jesus), she is chosen to carry the child of the father, but her life was given to Joseph to

---

[51] Pernell Hewing, Calling Forth The Bride of Christ For Intercession, (Whitewater, WI: Sanctuary Word Press, 1995).75

partner with (after the birth), to "raise" Jesus. "The Lord can, if he desires, choose to share you, His bride with an earthly mate of the Lords choosing… Because of your bridal relationship with the Lord, you can never choose a mate. Only the Lord can decide whether you will have a mate, and only the Lord can choose the mate."[52]

When my grandfather died (my father's father), I asked my grandmother, would she find another husband. She gave me a response that I had not heard before and do not remember hearing since. She said, "Darryl, God will be my husband." She has made her transition many years ago, and the statement was shared maybe 40 years ago now, but it still impacts me to this day. She eventually married a godly man (minister) after many years alone with God, and she never lost sight of her "bridal gown". "If you love The Bridegroom, Jesus Christ, with all your heart, He and He alone would have to make room for someone else to come into your heart and into your life. Know that there is no guarantee that He will ever allow anyone to come into your life to share that intimate love with you but Himself." Some will think you are "missing a few screws" in your head or say there is something strange about you. You may be called peculiar, weird, and [53] *even* "gay" (homosexual). Anyone who sells out *completely* to God, will find themselves under scrutiny; or intense criticism, from people who do not have a clue about what that means.

Father and Mother of Bridal Intercession

In the second chapter of Luke, we find the birth story of Jesus. Within the birth story, we get to meet two bridal intercessor types: Simeon and Anna (the Prophetess). Listen to the words of verses 28-38:

---

[52] Ibid. 76

[53] Ibid. 75

²⁸ Simeon took him in his arms and praised God, saying: ²⁹ "Sovereign Lord, as you have promised, you may now dismiss your servant in peace.³⁰ For my eyes have seen your salvation, ³¹ which you have prepared in the sight of all nations:³² a light for revelation to the Gentiles, and the glory of your people Israel."

³³ The child's father and mother marveled at what was said about him. ³⁴ Then Simeon blessed them and said to Mary, his mother: "This child is destined to cause the falling and rising of many in Israel, and to be a sign that will be spoken against, ³⁵ so that the thoughts of many hearts will be revealed. And a sword will pierce your own soul too."

³⁶ There was also a prophetess, Anna, the daughter of Penuel, of the tribe of Asher. She was very old; she had lived with her husband seven years after her marriage, ³⁷ and then was a widow until she was eighty-four. She never left the temple, but worshiped night and day, fasting and praying. ³⁸ Coming up to them at that very moment, she gave thanks to God and spoke about the child to all who were looking forward to the redemption of Jerusalem.

We do not know Simeon's marital status, but we do know about his devotion to the living of a righteous life, which cannot be attained or sustained without prayer. We know also, that he kept his nation in prayer, **expecting** the Christ to come. Here in this second chapter of Luke, verses 36 to 38 (that you just read) is the brief but powerful story of my favorite (bridal) intercessor. She is my hero of intercessory intimacy, consistency and commitment. She was married for seven (7) years. Her husband died, then she never left the Temple. It could very well be said of her that she *became* the temple. Talking about weird, peculiar, she had to be the epitome of it in the eyes of some. Can you imagine what they said about her? "She must be depressed", "lost it, hasn't she?" "What in the world?" "She is still there, are you serious?"

This kind of intercession is what I call "*enemy proof* intercession". It never ceases to fast and pray. There is no so called "catching" the true bridal intercessor off guard. His/Her lamp is ALWAYS "trimmed and burning." Their wedding attire is ALWAYS on, and fits properly. Bridal intercession is in essence "acting like I am already married, before the final ceremony." Is not that what is suppose to happen in the natural as well? All other dating ends when we get engaged to be married. There *are* no other prospects. My mind is made up and my heart is set on this one person and there is no turning around chasing or being chased and caught, by anyone else. I am standing side-by-side with Jesus, at *the* Father's right hand. What comes out of Jesus' mouth comes out of mine as well. Our hearts are one. Did you get that?

Real Men Do Not Wear a Dress, Or To They?

The obvious answer to that question is a resounding **No**! At least in the natural, we would never consider a ridiculous thought like this except in acting for a movie or some prank, disguise,(even then, most of us would have a problem). The closest thing to that I came to, was when I was in Europe a few years ago, visiting Scotland. We went into a clothing store and there I listened to the salesman as he served the men coming in and out of his suit shop. They were discussing wedding plans and I discovered that the traditional garb for men at a wedding, was the "Kilt". It is a "skirt like" outfit with bobby socks. It looked like something schoolgirls wear in the United States as their uniform (prep school). The salesman began to educate me, explaining to me the history of the "Kilt" and its use. I learned how versatile it was in its wear, being used as a jacket to cover you, or a blanket to sleep under for men who were traveling the rugged terrain. The color of the Kilt tells you whether it's for hunting, ancient, modern or a dress up one. Many families have their own colors. This is the national dress (for men) of Scotland and it is the official wear for weddings as our tuxedos would be in America. That all said, I tried one on and took pictures. It was a different look, but "sharp". I still *looked* like a man (all the time laughing as I was being fitted) and walked away saying, "okay that wasn't so bad, I could wear that to a wedding (if everybody else had one on).

    The problem men have, is the language we often use in church frightens our masculinity. The church is the "***bride***" of Christ. That however, is not a *gendered* term. No more is it than saying that we are the "*sons*" of God. In other words it simply says that we have the *spirit* of sonship. We are in the *image* of "the Son" of God. Does that make women "sons". In a sense, yes, but not as a gender, as an image, in the sight of the Father. Again, as Christians we walk in "Sonship" if we are in the image of Jesus.

    That said, when we speak of all of us (men include) as "the bride of Christ, we are not becoming effeminate or "girly" acting. We are merely putting on an image as well. The final scene is not about putting on a white wedding gown or a kilt, its being totally separated from the world and connected at the heart, to Jesus. *His* will and *my* will, have no detectable difference. Our wills are married, and match the will, heart desires of "the Father".

The Road To Marriage
The Five Steps Of Bridal Intercession

I.   The Call

    Revelation 19:7-9 [7] Let us rejoice and be glad and give him glory! For the wedding of the Lamb has come, and his bride has made herself ready. ⁸ Fine linen, bright and clean, was given her to wear." (Fine linen stands for the righteous acts of God's holy people.) ⁹ Then the angel said to me, "Write this: Blessed are those who are invited to the wedding supper of the Lamb!" And he added, "These are the true words of God."

The bridal call is an invitation to intimacy with the bridegroom. It is the wooing of the spirit of the bridegroom and the urging of the Father, to prepare for the eternal marriage ceremony. The summons to wed the heart of the church (the Christian), to the heart of Christ Jesus. It is the call to drown out the voice of every other lover, so that when the bridegroom speaks, he has no noteworthy competition. It is as if "E. F. Hutton" were speaking (an old commercial – when they spoke there was complete silence). The financial firm had a saying, "When E.F. Hutton talks, people listen."

Pernell Hewing writes, "The Bridal Love Call, calls you to open your heart wide for the love of Jesus to stream in and fill your life and guide you in every aspect of the Bridal Love Call. The Bridal Love Call is a call to refuse false attachments to people or things. The Bridal Call is a call for a love which will draw you gladly to a path of lowliness, of disgrace (disgrace in the world's eyes), and of obedience to Christ the Bridegroom, at all costs."⁵⁴

Solomon paints the picture of this "call" as he writes,
"¹⁰ My beloved spoke and said to me, "Arise, my darling, my beautiful one, come with me.
¹ See! The winter is past; the rains are over and gone. ¹² Flowers appear on the earth; the season of singing has come, the cooing of doves is

---

⁵⁴ Ibid. 82

heard in our land. ¹³ The fig tree forms its early fruit; the blossoming vines spread their fragrance. Arise, come, my darling; my beautiful one, come with me."
¹⁴ My dove in the clefts of the rock, in the hiding places on the mountainside, show me your face, let me hear your voice; for your voice is sweet, and your face is lovely." (Song of Solomon 2:10-14)

The question is this, Will you answer the call of the beloved? You my friend were made for *Him*. *You* were created for intimacy with God. Your intimacy will lead you to the place or position of intercession. *Intercession* is **the** birthing position. Pregnancy begins with intimacy. When intimacy is at its fullness, it births a heart for others. Your desire becomes set on helping birth them into their divine destiny. You long for the moment that they may also come to that special place with Christ Jesus.

When Jesus called the disciples, each one from a specific place in life, he called them away from their current *preoccupation* with their occupation. He called their attention ***away*** from things identified as "important/significant" in "*time,*" and ***to*** an understanding of prioritizing them, as it related to eternity. Did you get that? He changed their thinking. he set their mental state to operate in the realm of eternity. Stop thinking that the things of this world matter more than what is to come. He pursued *them*, so they could pursue *Him* and in turn teach others the worth of doing the same. What *is* the worth of pursuing Him, you ask? One word suffices, "PRICELESS!" The Call to Bridal Intercession is a priceless love call that is so intimate in nature, that it will literally cause you to weep just thinking about it. It *changes* you, **forever**.

II. The Choice

To be called by God is a privilege. I like watching draft days for basketball and football specifically, to see the look on players faces when they are drafted. There is so much excitement on *their* faces and their families, when seeing them chosen and sometimes called on the phone by a team owner or coach, welcoming them to the team. And yet, on some occasions, players have opted not to play for teams that have chosen them. All of the benefits offered could not sway them to change their mind. John Elway, who ended up a Denver Bronco, was like that when he found out that the Baltimore Colts (now of Indianapolis) were going to draft him. He set a tone. You have a choice.

Although there is no greater call, than to be called and chosen as a partner with Jesus, and to prepare others for eternal life, as opposed to eternal death, you still have a choice. He *proposes* to us, "Will you be my bride, my mate, my help meet, my lifesaver (in this case, *savior* of *His* body on the earth), my *destiny preparer?*" As we mentioned earlier, the Bridal intercessor is called, "The Priest/Nun" of Intercession. What I mean, is not that they *cannot* ever get married, but, that they *choose* intimacy (whether as a single man or woman or as a couple with the same focus) with Jesus as their number one priority and intense intercession, is a result of that.

Ephesians 1:3, 5 says that God chose *us* first.
"³ Praise be to the God and Father of our Lord Jesus Christ, who has blessed us in the heavenly realms with every spiritual blessing in Christ. ⁵ he predestined us for adoption to **sonship** through Jesus Christ, in accordance with his pleasure and will…"

Now, we like Saul of Tarsus, in his great transforming call found in Acts 9, must choose to answer, "Yes". Interestingly we should note, that there were two calls in that chapter. There was also the call of Annais, to intercede for Saul and disciple him into the leader he would become. He is one of the New Testaments' unsung heroes. Often, teachers do not get enough praise for what their students become. Intercessors also, are often unrecognized heroes in the earth, but God will not let them go unnoticed in heaven. The *Chief* intercessor (Jesus) has seen to that.

Years ago, as I heard the call of God on my life to preach the gospel, I answered it, but slowly I returned to my "vomit". What I saw in ministry lured me back to what I instinctively knew was spiritual infidelity. I walked in that "vomit" for more years than I like to remember. However, like Simon Peter in Luke 22:31, I heard the Lord say to me, Darryl, "Satan has desired to sift you as wheat, but **I** have PRAYED (interceded) for you. Now after you have been strengthened, strengthen the brothers." It was my *second* conversion, and I laid at the altar of our church for months, crying out to God, pursuing the pursuer. I understand Song of Solomon 3:1, 2 –

> "All night long on my bed I looked for the one my heart loves; I looked for him but did not find him. ²I will get up now and go about the city, through its streets and squares; I will search for the one my heart loves. So I looked for him but did not find him."

I wondered was I going to know Him, "in the power of His Resurrection" (and mine). Then, one day, it happened, he made himself known to me fully. Maybe it is better said that I finally recognized Him fully. I believe He was waiting, watching and wondering was I desperate for ***Him,*** or just what He ***had*** that I may use it to impress others. No, this time I was unmistakably certain, I wanted **Him**! My call was clear. I needed no mentors to impress or by which to be impressed. It was me and Jesus, introduced by Holy Spirit and the "Wedding" was On!

III. The Conviction

When we speak of conviction, we are talking about an unshakable belief that drives a person. The bridal intercessor must be convinced, that if they do not respond to the call to intercede for the "bride of Christ" and the world's preparation to meet the bridegroom, then the world will be lost, forever. Jesus *IS* coming. He *IS* going to judge the "quick and the dead". "It *IS* appointed unto man once to die and after that the judgment." (Hebrews 9:27) Guess what beloved, you and I *are* on the "eternity preparation team." We get to help prepare others for the wedding. Get this, we do not have the option to sit back and watch people populate hell and do nothing about it!

Conviction calls for a sense of urgency to fulfill assignments you are given. Jesus lived with conviction daily. His life was directed by "I musts". In Luke 2:49 he says, "I *must* be about my Father's business." Luke 4:43 records him saying, "I *must* preach the good tidings of the kingdom of God to other cities also; for therefore I was sent." John 9:4 records him saying, "As long as it is day, we *must* do the works of Him who sent me. Night is coming, when no one can work." John 4:4 records him saying, "He *must* needs pass through Samaria." Matthew 16:21 says, "From that time on Jesus began to explain to his disciples that He *must* go to Jerusalem and suffer many things at the hands of the elders, the chief priests and the teachers of the law, and that He *must* be killed and on the third day be raised to life."

The bridal intercessor lives the same "*must* do" life. "I *must* seek first the kingdom of God and His righteousness." "I *must* love God with all my heart and with all my soul and with all my mind." "I *must* bear the infirmities of the weak." "I *must* be about my Father's business." "I *must* love my enemies." "I *must* pray without ceasing." "I *must* keep myself unspotted from the world." Do not let that end your lists my beloved. Add to it. Do not allow it to keep you in bondage as just "strict laws", but principles you keep as an "engagement" promise you made to the Lamb (Jesus), in expectation of the great Wedding, because you love Him. In actuality, as we fore intimated, no *true* bride or groom, from the time of engagement, breaks their wedding vows, even though the actual marriage ceremony has not taken place, because there is a oneness/*wedding* of their hearts, first. The marriage feast is really a testimony of what God has *already* done in their hearts, just as the act of baptism is the public affirmation of a private commitment to totally submit, surrender one's life to Jesus.

III. The Commitment

The bridal intercessor, because of this conviction, commits him or herself to a life of purity. Hewing says, "The Bridal Call is a call to spend ones entire life for His/Her Bridegroom and the Bridegroom's wishes. His needs filled the bride so much that the bride's whole life is spent for the Bridegroom, doing what the Bridegroom directs." [55]

This kind of commitment will only be able to be accomplished with a lifestyle of fasting and praying. When Satan knows you have made the commitment to this level of intimacy he develops at least (3) things:

(1) Fear that you recognize your identity and will render him powerless;

(2) A fight strategy to distract you from having any kind of consistency with your Dominion status

(3) Frustration in your discipling assignment. Keep the disciples having their own issues, so that eventually you see them or the process you are going through as unproductive and therefore a waste of time.

---

[55] Ibid. 82

Before Jesus went to *begin* His earthly ministry and the whole time He *did* His ministering, He fasted and prayed. He knew, no flesh could be available for Satan to salivate upon. Satan exposes weaknesses and dines on doubt, for the world to see.

Esther's story in the Bible, is a brilliant example of commitment in preparation for the King. Vashti, the present Queen had violated her position and the King was in search for someone worthy to share his throne. After a nationwide search and invitation, many young, beautiful, talented women were called, chosen and accepted the call to present themselves before the King for his final approval. But before the final approval, 12 months of bathing and soaking in oils had to take place. Twelve months of "Queen training" had to be endured. This was no *ordinary* interview for a job. This was a *kingdom* ruling position that had to be meticulously prepared for, weeding out any impostors, good actors and flawed features that had been carefully hidden. If your heart was set on being the bride of the King, it would cost a great sacrifice of commitment. The greatest gift you can bring to Him is pure and proper preparation. "I Am Yours, Alone." Everyone else around me is there to assist me in serving, loving and honoring you.

IV. The Consolation

The groom IS coming! He will *not* stand us up, and it will be well worth the wait. The bridal intercessor, like others has to experience patience. The day of the Marriage Ceremony *Will* come and eternity with Him will be ours to enjoy.

Closing Thought

Gary Wiems writes,

"In my life, the primary result of spending extravagant amounts of time in the place of prayer, considering the beauty of the Lord, calling out to Him to establish His kingdom on the earth, has been the awakening of a yearning in my soul to be with Him face to face." [56]

That is the heart of a bridal intercessor. Seeing Him, adorned in all of His glory on that great day, is like only unto Christmas morning as a child. It is an "I CAN'T SLEEP!" like expectation, that inspires my life.

I challenge you my friend, to have that same expectation. The wedding is coming! The groom is dressed and looks immaculate. The bride needs to be prepared. You are the wedding planner as well as the bride. Don't sleep on your assignment. The bridegroom is depending on you!

---

[56] Gary Wiens, *Bridal Intercession: Authority in Prayer through Intimacy with Jesus* (Grandview, MO: Oasis House, 2001), 225

Chapter 10 The Family Intercessor

I really do not know what words to use to express to you how I feel about this area of intercession. It may be "THE" area that all the other areas surround and converge upon in this generation. The challenge of defining what a family is supposed to look like to this generation is tough. The biblical model of the family has seriously eroded and is being redefined by politicians, from the White House to the State Houses. It is largely going unchallenged by those who are carriers of, keepers of and proclaimers of the Word of God. The institution of marriage is being redefined. Fathers are absent and too often paying the penalty of two imprisonments. They are sent to jail for child support, which definitely does not benefit the child, and now *cannot* work at all. While they are imprisoned, their fees continue. When they are released we expect men who often did not have fathers to help them value things like family and discipline, to budget his time and money so that: 1) he can stay free and be able to earn income; and 2), he can help rear his children, spending time with them as well; and 3), still take care of his own needs. This is one of many serious and unaddressed issues in our society

We have not yet addressed the working mother, both married and/or single. Having to juggle the balls of marriage and job and household. Or, maybe just household, loneliness and rearing children.

Should we talk about the spirit of abandonment that rests in this generation, which is causing them to chase after the love of inanimate objects and a passion to socialize with themselves (video games) or screens with pictures and names of people we call friends, but have no meaningful relationships?

Should we address the staggering statistics of divorce in and out of the church and detail its effects on our children? Did you know that the Council on Civil Society in 1998 reported that strong, stable marriages were the seedbed of moral character and civic virtue and help build stronger, more stable, less violent communities? Did you know that married men and women generally live longer than single men and women? (American Journal of Sociology, 100:1131- 56). Did you know that the poverty rate for a child in a single-parent home is six times that of a married, two-parent home and that divorce often decreases the family income 37%? Did you know that statistics say, children from broken homes, when they become teenagers, have 2 to 3 times more behavioral and psychological problems than do children from intact homes? (Zill & Schoenborn 1998).

I know, all of these were a bit overwhelming. And yet, I haven't even scratched the surface. You, my friend, if you are serious about family intercession, your first assignment is to go and study the following areas so that you can know what you are truly assigned to do. It may begin with your family and a few people you know, but true intercessors always sense the calling beyond the limited boundaries of their own family and friends. Fighting for the healing and wholeness of others is our passion. One final stat: in a study done in Tennessee by First Things First, a nonprofit organization designed to rebuild, renew, and revitalize the city of Chattanooga, beginning with the family, found that 70% of the juvenile's in state reform institutions were from either a single or no parent home. There is something about the word "**family**" that should indicate "*protection*" and therefore needs to be "**protected**". So, my dear intercessors, what are you going to do about it? Here's your first assignment.

"Your Hands Can't Hit What Your Eyes Can't See"

Years ago, the great boxer Muhammed Ali had a little phrase he used to say "Float like a butterfly, sting like a bee, your hands can't hit what your eyes can't see". He was elusive and all his opponents knew it. He practiced deception or kept away from his opponents until he could tire them, frustrate them, then hit them with a knockout punch. That's what Satan does to us when we are uninformed. He keeps info from us, but good coaches, trainers are students of their adversaries or opponents. You have a better chance of beating opponents when you study their moves. So let's either get a researcher, or do it ourselves. Several things, are listed for you to consider. Let's go soldier!

Study The Decline of Marriage from the 1950s till now.

What affects has it had on society?

Study the incarceration of man, especially minorities.

What affects has it hand on their families?

Study the trend to legalize same-sex marriage.

Ask yourself and God, what affects this will have on society?

Study the history of abortion.

Do you know who Margaret Sanger is?

What are the effects of abortion on a woman?

What are the effects of abortions on men who have had a spiritual awakening/revelation on when life actually begins?

What effect does poverty have on family?

What are generational curses?

What is the number one cause of family breakup?

How does addiction affect the family? Incarceration? Mental illness?

What are the effects of sexual or physical abuse in the home?

I know, this seems like work does it not? Well of course it is! I told you already, you cannot be effective in prayer if you are not effective in understanding the seriousness of what you are praying about. The family is the reproducing vehicle of the world. If we lose it, we are doomed. Marriage, the *right* marriage, is designed to protect God's creation. It was designed for *image* reproduction. We were created in *His* image to re-create in *His* image. There are serious problems in the works of our present family life and an all out attempt to destroy the definition/description of marriage and family by restructuring it and painting an illegitimate image that has no fruit bearing potential in it. Dr. Tony Evans, writes, "In establishing the kingdom institution of the family, God created the expansion of his rule in history. That is precisely why Satan is trying to destroy the family. If Satan can destroy the family, he can destroy the expansion of God's Kingdom rule. Whoever owns the family owns the future."[57] Family intercessors are therefore protectors of the rulership of God. They are "warfare" intercessors with a specific assignment. They are warfare specialists. Stop Satan from establishing a rival kingdom in the

---

[57] Tony Evans, *Kingdom Man: Every Man's Destiny, Every Woman's Dream*, (Carol Stream, IL., Tyndale House), 2012, 164

earth, by protecting God's kingdom creating vehicle called family.

Reestablish The Standard

One of the hot topics of this generation is that of abortion and a woman's right to choose. The Pro-Life movement says there is no choice. The Pro-Choice movement says there should be, and then leaves it up to the woman, since it is her body. Well, maybe both of them are wrong. Is that possible? Well, yes, but in a strange way they are both right as well. Let me explain.

One of my sons in ministry and I were walking an exercise trail one morning when a couple appeared and gave us the thumbs up, saying, "Go Obama". I asked her why they had singled the only African-Americans out to share this. They stopped to engage us with why we should undoubtedly have been supporting the president, merely on the "culture issue". I was aghast, to say the least, at her presumption. While I think President Obama is very intelligent and has had an unusually difficult time in his unprecedented tenure in the Oval Office, I have been unashamedly opposed to two of his stances: same-sex marriage and abortion. Both of them threaten the very fiber of our society. They are principally contradictory to the Word of God.

I have addressed the marriage issue and now want to address the abortion issue. Neither of them are POLITICAL issues. They are moral STANDARD issues that Every intercessor must see clearly as an affront/assault on the Kingdom of God, no matter the source from which it comes. Eli died in the book of First Samuel, because he chose to ignore the sins of his sons Hophni and Phineas, choosing them, over God. We must choose God over All. When they disturbed Jesus, why he was teaching, to tell Him that His mother and brothers were at the door to see Him, He responded, "who are my mother and my brothers..."[58] he made it clear that this is bigger than blood, it's about the kingdom (establishing God Rule/Standards) in the Earth as it is in heaven.

Deuteronomy 30:19 (NIV) says, "This day I call the heavens and the earth as witnesses against you that I have set before you life and death, blessings and curses. Now choose life, so that you and your children may live." It is there where I want to address my previous statement about the right wing vs. left wing, Democrat vs. Republican, Elephants vs. Donkeys, continual controversy. God is pro-choice, as one of my sons and ministry says, "He just commands us to choose LIFE." Our bodies, on the contrary, are not our own. They are the temple of God. My body has been bought with a price. I live as a result of Jesus. I live for His glory, for His pleasure, to serve His Will and purpose in the earth. If He is my Lord, should I not ASK him for permission in all things, "What should I do?" If He has pre-existing standards already in place, should I not follow them, without being influenced by a political party? If the truth be told, we are a part of the party represented by the LAMB anyway, not an Elephant or a Donkey! Jesus, the Lamb of God, says in John 10:10 (NIV), "The thief comes only to steal and kill and destroy; I have come that they may have life, and have it to the full." He came that we might have Life – so then God is both Pro-Choice and Pro-Life, but His choice is that we be Life Producers and not death producers. The assignment of the family intercessor is to pray in **Life**!

Family Matters

Bernard Shaw, the American journalists, former news anchor at CNN is quoted as saying, "Perhaps the greatest social service that can be rendered by anybody to this country and to mankind is to bring up a family."[59] You my dear friend are the

---

[58] Matthew 12:48 NIV

[59] http://thinkexist.com/quotation//13459.html, Accessed June 19, 2013

catalyst for the birth of every family on earth. As a family intercessor your role is keeping the world alive. You are the seed planters in the spiritual realm that brings forth the harvest of right-thinking, right living and right creating. Let's look at some families in Scripture and see what we could glean from them to help you in your prayer time.

Adam and Eve

They portray for us the desire of our Father, for men to covenant with a wife and be fruitful. There is a sense of divine order in the choosing of a helpmeet exemplified in this story, even though God gave her to Adam. He did not desire him to be alone. In the book, *Dads: The Missing Link, Healing The Wounds Of A Generation,* I share that God is a God of order. "Just as in sports, when one is trying to live their life at a high level, there is a need for "order" or structure."[60] Men need to be interceded for so that they stay in divine order. When they are in order, their wives and children will have a living example standing before them. Here is a seven step process I prescribe in my book for every man to order his life by taken from Genesis, modeled after Adam.

1. God First – the creator of the universe; the giver of order; the ideal; the standard of good and right;

2. Gifts – something given that you did not earn or work for; special ability;

3. Goals- things which a person desires and works to accomplish in life;

---

[60] Darryl Husband, Dad: The Missing Link, Healing the Wounds Of A Generation, (Richmond, VA.,lulu.com 2012).74

4. Gig – slang word in the 60s and 70s for a job (the term is still used in music circles); work

5. Gal – the female gender that God created out of the rib of Adam (man) for the purpose of relationship, so man would not be alone and could populate the world

6. Gang – slang for family, the only real gang is the God-created family

7. Growth and Glow -- to continue to expand the spirit-man, so that God's Word and Will have an opportunity to shine in a dark world and people have a way to find Him.[61]

Adam forgot his assignment and caused Eves attention to wander, causing an interruption of cataclysmic nature. You do not have to have a clue about the far-reaching effect of *any* one act of your life. We will see that again in the life of Abraham.

A. For single people to wait for God to give them a soul mate

B. For strong men to head their households and be directed solely by God

C. For order and purpose in the life of men and women

D. For submission one to another (Ephesians 5:21)

---

[61] Ibid.,78

E. For intimacy and attention given one to another in marriage

F. Against infidelity, enemy invasion which produces eviction, divorce and a type of death.

G. The children of parents who have a disconnect with God, because they open themselves to jealousy, pride, anger, murder/destruction, inappropriate giving, lying, "Am I my brother's keeper" spirit, hiding sins and thinking God is blind.

Abraham and Sarah

They teach us several things to pray for as family intercessors.

A. To be led by God to where He wants them to live, work, set up their family lineage, legacy.

B. For strong faith to endure seasons of famine and unfulfilled promises. When Isaac didn't show up right away, they had to trust that God would STILL come through.

C. Pray for fruitfulness and barren women (wives)

D. Pray for the Spirit of Abraham/Hannah, to be upon our fathers and mothers and that they will be obedient to the offering of their children to God for His pleasure and not to pursue our broken or unfulfilled dreams.

Generational Curses

One of the definitions in Vines' Concise Dictionary of the Bible says that when a curse is on something, it is devoted to destruction.[62] A curse emanates from some sinful act or actions. The bible however, shows us how they can connect to one another. When sin enters and is not broken, it becomes a stronghold in a person's life. It then has the capability of removing God's hand of blessing or favor; protection or prosperity (peace, provisions etc.). An unbroken stronghold in a person's life can bring about a curse. The tragedy is that the curse can be inherited, passed down to generations (Exodus 20:5, which says, "⁵You shall not bow down to them or worship them; for I, the LORD your God, am a jealous God, punishing the children for the sin of the fathers to the third and fourth generation of those who hate me." [63]

Abraham left a "lying seed that Isaac and then grandson Jacob carried. David left a lust issue that killed his son Solomon, because he became addicted at another level."
"Now King Solomon loved many foreign women along with the daughter of Pharaoh: Moabite, Ammonite, Edomite, Sidonian, and Hittite women, ² from the nations concerning which the LORD had said to the sons of Israel, "You shall not associate with them, nor shall they associate with you, *for* they will surely turn your heart away after their gods." Solomon held fast to these in love. ³ He had seven hundred wives, princesses, and three

---

[62] Vine's Complete Expository Dictionary of Old and New Testament Words ,1984, 1996, Thomas Nelson, Inc., Nashville, TN, pg 53

[63] Darryl Husband, *Living a Lifestyle of Fasting* (Richmond: lulu.com, 2011),72

hundred concubines, and his wives turned his heart away. ⁴For when Solomon was old, his wives turned his heart away after other gods; and his heart was not wholly devoted to the LORD his God, as the heart of David his father *had been.*"(I Kings 11:1-4 NASB)

When looking at the lives of Jacob, Rachel and Leah, David (his wives), and Solomon and his wives, there is so much for family intercessors to learn from to use as we pray for this generation. Let's look at some biblical characters that you can use to ensure that you get in the mindset of looking at every couple and family in the Bible, as a springboard for family intercession. A look at these biblical characters will give us divine revelation of the needs in any generation.

Jacob, Rachel and Leah

Pray about the devotion of every husband to one wife and every wife to one husband.

Pray about healing the wounds that absentee father's cause.

Pray about breaking the spirit of jealousy.

Pray for men to recapture chivalry, respecting the parents of his wife to be enough to request the hand of their daughter in marriage.

Pray for the desire of men to be priests, providers, protectors and pointers towards divine destiny in their homes.

Pray Ephesians 5:22 – 23 which says, "[22] Wives, submit yourselves to your own husbands as you do to the Lord. [23] For the husband is the head of the wife as Christ is the head of the church, his body, of which he is the Savior."

Pray Colossians 3:18 – 21 which says, "[18] Wives, submit yourselves to your husbands, as is fitting in the Lord. [19] Husbands, love your wives and do not be harsh with them. [20] Children, obey your parents in everything, for this pleases the Lord. [21] Fathers, do not embitter your children, or they will become discouraged."

Pray Ephesians 6:1 -4 which says, "Children, obey your parents in the Lord, for this is right. [2] "Honor your father and mother"— which is the first commandment with a promise— [3] "so that it may go well with you and that you may enjoy long life on the earth."[4] Fathers, do not exasperate your children; instead, bring them up in the training and instruction of the Lord."

Pray Deuteronomy 6:1 – 8 which says, "These are the commands, decrees and laws the LORD your God directed me to teach you to observe in the land that you are crossing the Jordan to possess, [2] so that you, your children and their children after them may fear the LORD your God as long as you live by keeping all his decrees and commands that I give you, and so that you may enjoy long life. [3] Hear, Israel, and be careful to obey so that it may go well with you and that you may increase greatly in a land flowing with milk and honey, just as the LORD, the God of your ancestors, promised you.

⁴ Hear, O Israel: The LORD our God, the LORD is one⁵ Love the LORD your God with all your heart and with all your soul and with all your strength. ⁶ These commandments that I give you today are to be on your hearts. ⁷ Impress them on your children. Talk about them when you sit at home and when you walk along the road, when you lie down and when you get up. ⁸ Tie them as symbols on your hands and bind them on your foreheads.

Pray Proverbs 22:3 –9 which says, "The prudent see danger and take refuge, but the simple keep going and pay the penalty. ⁴ Humility is the fear of the LORD; its wages are riches and honor and life. ⁵ In the paths of the wicked are snares and pitfalls, but those who would preserve their life stay far from them. ⁶ Start children off on the way they should go, and even when they are old they will not turn from it. ⁷ The rich rule over the poor, and the borrower is slave to the lender. ⁸ Whoever sows injustice reaps calamity, and the rod they wield in fury will be broken. ⁹ The generous will themselves be blessed, for they share their food with the poor.

David/Bathsheba/Abigail/Michel

Pray for the breaking of any lingering flesh issues in the lives of husbands or wives which link them to old habits that cause their eyes to wander

Pray Job 31:1-4 which says, ""I made a covenant with my eyes not to look lustfully at a young woman. ² For what is our lot from God above, our heritage from the Almighty on high? ³ Is it not ruin for the wicked, disaster for those who do wrong? ⁴ Does he not see my ways and count my every step?

Pray for fathers to protect their daughters from predators

Pray for wives (Abigail) to speak to and nurture the King in their husbands and discourage the fool in them.

Pray for wives (Bathsheba) to stand strong when their husbands are absent, or not paying attention and strong man are prowling and luring them away from their covenant.

Pray for wives and husbands (Michal, daughter of Saul), to break the apron strings of their parents and cling to one another, celebrating one another's joys, mourning and cherishing one another in defeats and sorrow.

Solomon

Pray for wisdom, not just to lead others, but to lead themselves.

Pray for the strength to finish strong in marriage, not to get weary. Many marriages go through struggles. Pray that couples work through their many stages. (Financial, communication, empty nest etc.)

Pray for marriages to be built on the right principles.

"The chain of disaster is clear. The homes devoid of regular working or continuous care, lead directly to insecurity and delinquency on the part of the young. These in turn set up homes where a similar pattern is demonstrated. How shall we break this vicious chain? Before we can break it we take need to know the nature of the trouble. Part of the trouble is, of course, economic, but by no means all. A good share of the trouble is moral and, if we go beyond the surface, most of it may be. One of the chief reasons why so many habitations are not homes is that other things are prized more."[64]

Elton and Pauline Trueblood wrote these words some 60 years ago and they are as applicable today as they were then. Truth never dies! It may be silenced, amid the noise of the *current day*, but it cannot be continually ignored.

My Story

Even good families experience bad results at times. Why? Because good does not mean perfect. My twin sister and younger brother and I were reared in a Christian home with two college graduate parents who were both loving and nurturing. They disciplined us (the old-fashioned way) and developed in us an understanding about success in life, and the work ethics needed to achieve it. We were learned to cook, clean, value money, family, God (not in that order). We were

---

[64] Elton Trueblood, Patricia Trueblood. *The Recovery Of Family Life*. New York, NY: Harper & Brothers. 1953, 31

monitored carefully in regards to friendships/relationships, so we did not become attached to the wrong crowds. We all were sent to the "right" schools and were directed towards good careers. We had a "Good" family.

However, all of us experienced things in our lives that we would have to admit, we are un-proud of: be it drugs; alcohol; premarital sex; incarceration; child out of wedlock. Proverbs 22:6 is so appropriate. We should train our families in the way they should go. The job of the parent is simple; give direction! That appears to be the assignment that parents have lost sight of. When take care of that assignment there is a foundation in place. As the children go, they will find their way back to their roots. We all did (my sister, brother and I all did).

Good families are all around, but *good* can always be better. As I think about my own family (then and now), there is always room for improvement. My parents didn't teach us *how* to pray, but they took us to the place where we practiced praying (the Church).

My job is to teach my children *how* to pray and eventually *why* we pray. In all of what my wife and I try to do, I am certain when our children look back, they will discover things we *didn't* do or teach them to do as well. We are all human and miss things, that's why we need FAMILY Intercessors. Family intercessors pray for us when we cannot see what we need to see. You are NEEDED. Do not sleep on the job.

Final Thought

As you intercede my friend, know that my life and the lives of every family in the world is being impacted by your heart and your words. You have the power to shape, reshape the first great institution God created. I leave you with this: " The natural family is the foundational unit, inscribed in human nature and centered around the voluntary union of a man and a woman in a lifelong covenant of marriage for the purpose of:

- satisfying the longings of the human heart to give and receive love

- welcoming and ensuring the full physical and emotional development of children

- sharing a home that serves as a center for social, educational, economic and spiritual life

- building strong bonds among the generations to pass on a way of life that has transcending meaning

- and extending a hand of compassion to individuals and households whose circumstances fall short of these ideals"[65] (World Congress of Families II, Geneva 1999, A Call From The Families Of The World)

---

[65] Bridget Mahar editor, *The Family Portrait*, Family Research Council, Washington, DC, 2004

Chapter 11 The Soul/Salvation Intercessor

Okay, if you're reading this chapter, then I must admit, I am encouraged. If the truth be told, in many churches today, the buzzwords are centered around buildings and budgets, to entice "fish" from "other aquariums." Have you listened to the marketing strategies today? We advertise: screens; technology; gadgets; personalities; and performances. People are running from one church to the next to see the latest social media, religious "star." We have cast our nets in the wrong places and found ourselves luring fish that have already been caught.

In the second chapter of Matthew, there is recorded the story of the Magi that came to Jerusalem asking, "Where is the one who has been born King of the Jews? We saw his star in the East and have come to worship him."(Matthew 2:2 NIV). Make no mistake about it, when *we* have become the "star", we miss *the* Star. We must restore Jesus to *His* rightful place. With that, He will redirect His church to its purpose. Soul winning is a mandate, not a request. His training of the disciples was about making them "fishers of men." The assignment of the soul intercessors is to first pray for the conversion of the **church**. The gospel of Luke, records Jesus saying to Simon Peter, "Simon, Simon, Satan has asked to sift you as wheat. But I have prayed for you, Simon, that your faith may not fail. And when you have turned back, strengthen your brothers (Luke 22:31, 32 NIV). We must pray for one another that our eyes be reopened to the purpose for which we were birthed.

Divine Obsession

Since the fall of man, (chapter 3 of Genesis), God has had one focus: restore His people to their place of dominion. He has sent prophets, priests, kings, apostles, evangelists, pastors, teachers, elders, diaconate and His only Son. He illustrates this in several places in scripture, but never more graphic is His love for us seen than the story of Hosea and Gomer. "Hosea, whose name means "salvation", had a unique role as a prophet of God. Unique in large part because God asked Hosea to do something he never asked anyone to do before (or after). He asked the prophet to marry a prostitute. Yep, you read that right. Not a former prostitute, but a full-fledged, card-carrying active prostitute. It definitely sounds insane. Ludicrous. It is! And that's the point-it compels us to notice God's Divine Obsession with his children."[66]

Without a doubt, we are giving a panoramic view of the heart of God for lost humanity. He is aware of our cheating heart. He knows all of the distasteful details about our past and present. He is acquainted with how deep our addiction to every proclivity we have. Despite this, he still loves us and desires to save us from our sinful life. He was, is, and forever will be convinced, that we were made for Him. Nothing will change that, even if we choose not to accept it.

In the gospel of Luke Chapter 19, a story is recorded of a tax collector whose name was Zaccheaus. He was called, "chief" tax collector. This may indicate seniority or longevity on the job, which would categorize him in the community as a long time enemy or "super thief." He was indeed , a hated, marked man. The people called him a sinner, but Jesus labels him a prospect, a candidate, for the kingdom of God. Lets watch and listen in on Zaccheaus as he responds to the request Jesus makes to come to his house. As Zaccheaus comes down

---

[66] Jud Wilhite, *Pursued: God's Divine Obsession with You* (New York: FaithWords, 2013), 17

to accept the invitation and walks Jesus to his house, people grumble, acknowledging his obvious life as a sinner. But even while the people were grumbling: "... Zaccheaus stopped and said to the Lord, behold, Lord, half of my possessions I will give to the poor, and if I have defrauded anyone of anything I will give back four times as much. And Jesus said to him, today salvation has come to this house because he too, is a son of Abraham. For the Son of Man has come to seek and to save that which was lost." (Luke 19:8-10 NASB)

It is apparent to me, Jesus is interested in souls. He will not be distracted by naysayers. He is our high priest, our chief intercessor. The assignment of the soul (salvation) intercessors is to take all of their desires and direct them towards praying in the harvest of lost men, women, boys and girls, in spite of their background.

The Word

If you are a soul/salvation intercessor, you have to have the heart of *the* Father. Daily you labor before the throne of God on behalf of the lost. Your life mission is found in II Peter 3:9, 10, which says,

> "[9] The Lord is not slow in keeping his promise,
> as some understand slowness. Instead he is
> patient with you, not wanting anyone to perish,
> but everyone to come to repentance. [10] But the
> day of the Lord will come like a thief. The
> heavens will disappear with a roar; the elements
> will be destroyed by fire, and the earth and
> everything done in it will be laid bare.

You have determined that not one soul in the world will spend eternity in hell if you have anything to say about it.

Man is a living breathing soul, infiltrated by a former heavenly being, who is seeking to establish his own kingdom after an effort of coup d'état (to overthrow) the kingdom of heaven. He has not ceased with his desire. He failed in heaven.

He has not changed. he has always had and now has the same desire: "to be god" in the earth. He desires to set up his own system of government or way of ruling. He loves darkness, chaos, confusion, destruction and death. His weapons are many, but I believe his favorites are: discouragement; distraction; doubt; and delay.

Discouragement

A huge area of prayer today needs to be targeted in the area of discouragement. This "millennial" generation is the first generation to really begin to experience life without a plethora of good male role models in their intimate space. Because of this, they in many ways do not even know that they are discouraged, deprived of courage and hope. In areas of their lives where males were designed to impart significant life directing things, many of those males were absent. Therefore, tragically I believe there has been a generation wide imbalance. Of course, all have not suffered this, but when we research the statistics of the family today, we see the overall results, agree with my conclusion (do the research on single parenting).

Discouragement has its root in fear. It does not believe it has what it takes to succeed. It lacks cheerleaders to push trying something again and again. Cheerleaders or supporters are there to at least make you believe that your *failings*, do not a *failure,* make. It is quitting before completing what you set out to do and choosing not to return to it, that may label one a failure. It is ceasing to make every effort to achieve ones goals and in essence not caring anymore. What we do not realize enough, is that *failings* have two options linked to them: (1) they help us learn to succeed if we use them properly; and (2) they *also* make us run and hide, if no one is there to say, "try it again! Yes you can do this! I believe in you!"

Distraction/Deception

Have you ever noticed that when you are on a real mission for God, all sorts of things, people and places to go, evolve from the "wood works"? Some of those things you really want to do, but know it's bad timing and you have to fight them off. Today, everything demands our time as no other era in history. We are distracted by phones that are often attached to our hands as though they were a part of our body. iPads, Notebooks, Nooks, iPods, iPhones, Blackberry's, the latest android, smart, smarter, smartest phone, all keeping us occupied, often without really talking verbally to anyone. We now have a generation that has an intimacy with and an addiction to, inanimate objects. People are actually getting counseling for it.

This may seem like a strange analogy, but have you ever noticed, that the symbol for Apple technology is a "bitten apple"? "Eye candy", technological genius has given us a mental "sweet tooth" and attracts our attention calling us to it religiously. It has replaced books, libraries, and in some places even "The Bible". It reminds me of the movie "The Book Of Eli", starring Denzel Washington. The most precious, priceless, cherished thing in their society, after its destruction, was a Bible. Eli had the only copy left on earth. It was his life goal to deliver it somewhere where it could be kept and duplicated, so humankind could once again build on its principles. Beware my beloved, tis true, if you want a glimpse of the future, watch the movies. Life very often does imitate art.

Genesis 3, is a story of distraction and deception. The food and fruit was used as both. It was painted as *so good-looking*, that one should never ignore it, and eventually be enticed to consume it. It was the beginning of a takeover. The distraction however, began with the life attention or lack thereof, that Adam gave to Eve. When "Soul" intercessors are distracted by other less important things, nations die. It is extremely important that soul intercessors are not so worldly driven or easily attracted to things. They cannot be childish in behavior. Children are always chasing toys, games, colors and sweets, with no concept of time (or eternity for that matter).

Doubt

Genesis 3 is also where we find the spirit of doubt. "Now the serpent was more crafty than any of the wild animals the Lord had made, and he said to the woman, did God really say: You must not eat from any tree in the garden?" Now her response was correct. But the problem was, she started a conversation with a deceiver and his goal began with an introduction question that infused doubt. However, doubt was merely the beginning. The purpose of the doubt was to conclude with eviction from the presence of God. in other words it had as its desired end, "eternal excommunication".

Delay

"Wait", the enemy of our soul says, "Wait until you are older." "Wait until next Sunday." "Wait until your spouse is ready." "You have time. You're having too much fun." "You are too young to totally commit your life to anything." "God is patient, don't rush this thing." Does anyone know the day they will die? If you do not know the day you are going to die, then delay is not an option. The soul/salvation intercessor must pray a spirit of "urgency" into this and every generation to come.

The Womb

The Soul/Salvation Intercessor is always watching the Church, "universal" for its integrity, intimacy, intentions and interests. They pray for the place where spiritual infants are born and/or nurtured. The church is in the world to produce and maintain a perpetual pregnancy. It must *never* be barren. Its purpose is to deliver babies and mature them to become producers of the same.

Elizabeth Alves says, "Soul intercessors need to be the ones up front when the altar call is given. They should ensure that those who come to the Lord are given the good milk of the Word and when needed, warm living arms to comfort them. Part of the birthing experience involves making sure the new babies are passed on to loving shepherds."[67] while I agree with that, I must caution you to ask your pastor where you should be, before you start moving from your seat. *Your* place, is where you are assigned. You can obviously be a powerful image before the people and close by the delivery room by standing up front, but it's not just about standing in a place, as much as it is about *"BEING"* in place. God can hear your prayers from your seat, just make certain you are praying. Pastor Rick Warren is quoted as saying in his book purpose driven life, ""when God has a bunch of baby believers he wants to deliver, he looks for the warmest incubator church he can find.." [68]

The Warning

Soul intercessors have to have in their hearts a constant desire to pray and/or cry out to God for the sins of the world. We are praying that God will send warning signs and people, to help every lost person understand the consequences of sin. We are mindful that in our society today, it is becoming easier and easier not to talk about the consequences of sin. We must pray for the fivefold ministry gifts (apostles, prophets, evangelists, pastors, teachers) and every leader in the body of Christ, to be convinced, convicted, persuaded by Holy Spirit, to keep Romans 3:23, "for all have sinned and fall short of the glory of God," at the forefront of their thinking, as we reach out and train others for kingdom service.

---

[67] Alves *Intercessors*, 67

[68] Rick Warren, *The Purpose-Driven Life: What On Earth Am I Here For?* (Grand Rapids, Mich.: Zondervan Publishers, 2002),167

John, had a theme in his preaching. He knew that his assignment was one of preparing people for the coming of the Lord. One word became his trademark or calling cry, "Repent"! This is at the heart of every prayer meeting for soul intercessors, that people, who are lost, will hear, see, or experience something, that would cause them to repent. We are busy today calling people to come as they are, and of course accepting them as they are because we love them. This is great, but it is only the first stage of the process. Jesus called Matthew the tax collector and Peter the rambunctious fisherman just as they were, but he spent three years training their spirit man to dominate their flesh. He desired them to overcome every worldly way of thinking and acting. He was not interested in merely "growing the size of the church" in the earth. That is window dressing. He was interested in saving souls for eternity.

Listen to the words carefully in John 6:53," Jesus said to them, "Very truly I tell you, unless you eat the flesh of the Son of Man and drink his blood, you have no life in you." This passage looks at first glance like something to use as a "communion" passage. However, upon closer investigation, it sounds like Jesus is really saying, "your life should be just like mine when I finish with you." "You should be dead to your old way of living and alive in my way. Go back to how we made the original man and woman." Then in versus 60 to 66 he finds out who is with him and who is not, as the disciples begin to wrestle with the difficulty of total transformation and not just surface salvation.

> [60] Therefore many of His disciples, when they heard *this* said, "This is a difficult statement; who can listen to it?" [61] But Jesus, conscious that His disciples grumbled at this, said to them, "Does this cause you to stumble? [62] *What* then if you see the Son of Man ascending to where He was before? [63] It is the Spirit who gives life; the

flesh profits nothing; the words that I have spoken to you are spirit and are life. ⁶⁴ But there are some of you who do not believe." For Jesus knew from the beginning who they were who did not believe, and who it was that would ⁽ⁱ⁾betray Him. ⁶⁵ And He was saying, "For this reason I have said to you, that no one can come to Me unless it has been granted him from the Father." ⁶⁶ As a result of this many of His disciples withdrew and were not walking with Him anymore. (John 6:60-66 NASB)

There is a warning, whaling, prayer cry, that soul intercessors must have on behalf of the world. That, is a given. However, there *is* a warning that all *soul* intercessors are given as well. Two passages of scripture come to mind: Jonah's calling; and Ezekiel's calling.

Are You Serious Lord?

Jonah could not believe God would even desire to save Nineveh, let alone call him to intercede for them. I mean, "What is He thinking?" "Does He know these people are the scum of the earth?" "I will *not* go!" And at the outset he did not. He headed in an opposite direction. When you read Jonah, you see his obstinance caused his obstacles. When you are called by God to intercede, you pay for your negligence, and so do the people on board the boat in which your life is traveling. Fulfill your assignment!

Keep Your Hands Clean!

"¹⁶ At the end of seven days the Word of the LORD came to me, saying, ¹⁷ "Son of man, I have appointed you a watchman to the house of Israel; whenever you hear a word from My mouth, warn them from Me. ¹⁸ When I say to the

> wicked, 'You will surely die,' and you do not warn him or speak out to warn the wicked from his wicked way that he may live, that wicked man shall die in his iniquity, but his blood I will require at your hand. ¹⁹ Yet if you have warned the wicked and he does not turn from his wickedness or from his wicked way, he shall die in his iniquity; but you have delivered yourself. (Ezekiel 3:16-19 NASB)

It is not the job of the prophet, intercessor, evangelist or apostle to judge whether they should pray, warn or prepare people, based upon "*THEM*". The people have NOTHING to do with our decision to intercede. It is ALL about the call. The question for you, is "Will your hands be dirty or clean at the end of each day?"

The Workers

Soul/Salvation intercessors are lifeguards. They guard against the premature death of every person in the world. They refuse to see a life aborted, handed over to eternity, before it is truly born (again) and experiencing the God kind of life.

Alves, Femrite and Kaufman call souls/salvation intercessors our "spiritual midwives". The responsibilities of a midwife are varied, but they all center around the safe delivery and immediate aftercare of babies. Their job is to help the mother bring forth children. They are called to stand in the gap to push the mother to fulfill the purpose for which she was born.

"God's spiritual midwives move in deep anguish for souls to be born. They prayerfully stand in the gap between two kingdoms as lighthouses for those who are lost in the kingdom of darkness, directing them into the kingdom of light."[69]

---

[69] Alves, Intercessors, 56

The words of Jesus ring loudly in my ears, even as I write these words, "The harvest is plentiful, but the workers are few. Ask the Lord of the harvest, therefore, to send out workers into his harvest field."(Matthew 9:37, 38 NIV). These words were written long ago and have the danger of being overlooked, because there are so many people in the world who are professing Christians. However, in spite of the number of churches in many of our cities and counties, the number of people truly committed to soul winning is not great.

It might sound strange to many, but things are shifting, and have been for a while. I was in a prayer service recently for the National Day of Prayer (USA) and a brother from Vietnam was present. He was asked to speak to us before we dismissed. His words were confirmation to a conclusion I made several years ago. I came to the conclusion that America was in a spiritual war that it was losing. The spirit of tolerance had entered our culture and has been affirmed by the president when he said that we were no longer a Christian nation, but one of many religions. He was reported as saying that he thought we should join a debate on how to reconcile faiths, with the pluralistic society we live in. We have been infiltrated by every religious sect in the world, while in the countries where some of the religions come from, they will kill a relative or disown them, for becoming a Christian. How did they come to live at peace in a Christian nation, yet believing that the people who live here are "infidels", worthy of death (like their converted loved one), unless of course the purpose is a tactical, subtle siege of the society.

The gentleman from Vietnam said to us, "Brothers and sisters, I am not a refugee here in America, I am a missionary." WOW! So those we once went to preach the gospel to, are now coming to save us. They see that we are drowning in our own prosperity. We are killing ourselves with pride, greed, anger, abuse, "family destroying" policies. The mission *center* has become the mission *field*. Intercessors, Pray for harvest workers!

List Of Laborers to Pray For

1. Missionaries: home and foreign

2. Soul Intercessors-that they do not become weary in well doing.

3. Evangelists-to live lives of integrity

    - Discipline their time so they can pray and study the word.

    - Use the right communication tools for every setting they are in

4. Revival starters to break out in our land; churches; cities; personal and corporate

5. Revivals /Conferences/Crusades-healing gifts to move without fear and devoid of   the purposes of men

6. Financial investors

7. Sunday Service/Workers- people not so much in a hurry to leave church but making it a priority. When we were in the world we never got enough. Time was a non factor. Why is it that we come to the kingdom of God and want to hurry back to the world. "Church is too long". Was the party? Ever? You may have something *else* to do, but nothing *better*.

8. Outreach Teams-in communities often for visibility (the church is often too in-reach focused)

    - every church needs a plan for outreach focused on some need the community has and not just a "church project" to say we did something.

9. Research team to discover the community's needs: physical; emotional; financial; and spiritual

10. Visionaries-to constantly see the end and encourage the Saints on this journey

11. Disciple makers-once the souls come, we need people who can grow them to maturity

12. Caregivers-big Brothers/sisters

- deacons
- small group leaders
- leaders of ministries

Do not let this list be exhaustive. Add every worker you can think of to this list,

The Work

Have you ever noticed that atheist do not take a day off? What about Satan worshipers? Soothsayers? Palm readers? You cannot even imagine one of them waking up in the morning saying, "You know what? I feel like acting like Jesus today, giving God glory." That will not happen. So, since they do not take a break, why do we? We should never let Satan and his kingdom entourage outwork us. They cannot outperform, out pray, or out penetrate our kingdom.

Souls are won to the Kingdom of God by a process. That process has a beginning and an ending to it. And yet, there is no end to the beginning and no ending to the end. In other words the work of salvation does not end while there is *one* soul left on the earth, that has not heard the gospel of Jesus Christ. Here is my five (5) step process

1. Birthed by Prayer-John 17:20-23 NASB "[20] "I do not ask on behalf of these alone, but for those also who believe in Me through their word; [21] that they may all be one; even as You, Father, *are* in Me and I in You, that they also may be in Us, so that the world may believe that You sent Me.[22] The glory which You have given Me I have given to them, that they may be one, just as We are one; [23] I in them and You in Me, that they may be perfected]in unity, so that the world may know that You sent Me, and loved them, even as You have loved Me.

Jesus prays in the John 17 passage, for the present and the future disciples who would come to know him and all of his glory. We should be praying in the same manner. When Jesus said (Matthew 28:19) for the disciples to "go" into all of the world, we should take that as a prayer assignment. Pray for a *"going spirit"* in the body of Christ. Pray for every Christian to be obedient to the call of the great commission.

Finally, if the Lord of the harvest has the ability to send effective workers into the world, to bring forth the great harvest of souls, why aren't we seeking his help?

> "35 Jesus was going through all the cities and villages, teaching in their synagogues and proclaiming the gospel of the kingdom, and healing every kind of disease and every kind of sickness. 36 Seeing the people, He felt compassion for them, because they were distressed and dispirited like sheep]without a shepherd. 37 Then He said to His disciples, "The harvest is plentiful, but the workers are few. 38 Therefore beseech the Lord of the harvest to send out workers into His harvest." Matthew 9:35 NASB

One could say that these were not lost souls, but who knows? What we do know is, that whenever sick people got healed or possessed people receive deliverance, they followed Jesus and told it everywhere they went. Their testimonies brought people into the Kingdom of God. Then, souls are:

2. Baited By Passionate Persistence – John 4:3, 4- ³ He left Judea and went away again into Galilee. ⁴ And He had to pass through Samaria.

This is an unusual word, because Jews avoided Samaria and Samaritans like we would the plague or flu "bug". However, his encounter with this woman who is without a doubt considered as an outcast among the outcasts, is the seed for a great harvest of souls. She was lured in with the bait of *"passionate persistence"*. While she was trying to give Jesus the "brush-off", he would not take NO for an answer. You my dear intercessor, BE PERSISTENT, PASSIONATELY PERSISTENT, in your prayer time, about the people who look like they are saying "No" to Christ. Do not give up on them! Especially those that do not *look like* you, or may be outside of your culture. You do not have a clue, except from the story, what effect, your efforts will have. Listen to the end result of the bait of "passionate persistence":

> ³⁹ From that city many of the Samaritans believed in Him because of the word of the woman who testified, "He told me all the things that I *have* done." ⁴⁰ So when the Samaritans came to Jesus, they were asking Him to stay with them; and He stayed there two days.
> ⁴¹ Many more believed because of His word;
> ⁴² and they were saying to the woman, "It is no longer because of what you said that we believe, for we have heard for ourselves and know that

this One is indeed the Savior of the world." (John 4:39-42 NASB)

Then those souls are:

3. Benefited By Partnership – Acts 2:42, 47 (NASB) ^{42} They were continually devoting themselves to the apostles' teaching and to fellowship, to the breaking of bread and to prayer. ^{47} praising God and having favor with all the people. And the Lord was adding to their number day by day those who were being saved.

There was a unity of purpose amongst the believers. Let us do what we do with a single focus. We can cause God to respond to us with favor, and men to respond by surrendering their lives.

Soul intercessors must believe, that as they connect with other soul intercessors, that heaven backs it and earth shifting things begin to happen. 3000 souls were saved in a day. Talking about increase! Do it again Lord!

Then souls are:

4. Blessed by Perceptivity – Acts 9:32 (NASB) Now as Peter was traveling through all *those regions*, he came down also to the saints who lived at Lydda

The assignment of the soul intercessor is to pray for the gift of the evangelist (as well as every member of the body of Christ), to stay in a mode of discernment. Every Christian should know that when they are perceptive about what is going on around them and the real needs of people, not just seeing their *outer* shell, and making a judgment based on it. It is the art of looking on the situation and being able to see potential not just present position. The intercessors job is to help ignite potential, putting it in position to participate in the life of a person so they can operate on a higher level than they are presently.

Peter sees this man who looks like he is a permanent fixture of poverty and failure. He reaches more than his hand, but he touches his heart. The miracle begins. The once lame man then reaches out to bring the souls of two cities to the Lord Jesus Christ. Never take for granted the ability of another because of their present condition. Pray, intercessors, that not one member of the body forgets to exercise the power of expectation in the life of those who have an empty appearance.

Then finally, souls we are praying to reach are:

5. Blocked By Petty People – III John 9-11 (NASB) ⁹I wrote something to the church; but Diotrephes, who loves to be first among them, does not accept [f]what we say. ¹⁰ For this reason, if I come, I will call attention to his deeds which he does, unjustly accusing us with wicked words; and not satisfied with this, he himself does not receive the brethren, either, and he forbids those who desire *to do so* and puts *them* out of the church. ¹¹ Beloved, do not imitate what is evil, but what is good. The one who does good is of God; the one who does evil has not seen God.

Whatever you do, please do not forget that you are at war. We are always aware that souls are going to be hindered from coming into the body of Christ by outside influence. However, we must pray as well for protection against the enemy ***within***. There will always be people who are inside of the house of God or better yet, the fellowship, who like the man in III John, make every effort to win souls and mature saints as frustrating as they possibly can. Soul intercessors must pray to destroy the spirit of Diotrophes.

In his letters to the churches, Paul calls the names of several people who needed watching, so that they did not block the flow of growth. e.g. Roman 16:17; II Timothy 4:14.

Several years ago, I was in a class with a pastor who was in quite a dilemma. He had a heart for souls. Of course, that was not the dilemma. You see, he pastored a very aristocratic, "silk stocking", church, but it was located in a neighborhood that had become poverty-stricken. The pastor, noticing the members were not winning souls, suggested to do a community campaign. To his surprise the members went into temper tantrums. They made it clear, "We do **not** want those kind of people in **our** church." I wonder, "what is heaven going to look like?" Will we have segregation there? Color lines? Classism? I think not!

Soul intercessors must break the pitiful, petty posture of people who believe the church belongs to them.

People Groups - That Salvation May Come To Them

The Jews- Roman 10:

The Gentiles

Religions

Atheists

Lost Sheep- Outside and inside of House of God

Carnal Crowd- Inside

The Wait

"Our responsibility is not to change others; it is to pray the circumstances will be aligned so that they have the opportunity to choose. When we enter into prayer for souls, we enter into Christ suffering. He died for all. But not everyone will receive his gift of salvation, and that truth is painful. Our responsibility is to continue to go and tell until all have heard!"[70]

---

[70] Ibid. 70

This is true, we must tell the gospel story until all have heard, and it is also true that we cannot stop interceding until the "tellers" *and* the telling, is complete. Soul intercessors intercede like unto the Lord, as he prayed in the Garden of Gethsemane until drops of blood emerge from his pores. Can you see that? Your cross is found on your knees. Your heart should never stop bleeding for the loss.[71]

Daily Duties

1. Awaken With Personal Devotion Time-stay clean and confident

2. Keep A Souls Journal-a list of the lost and found

3. Pray For Laborers-"some plant, some water… God gives the increase

4. Expect God To Respond-"Father I know you always hear me…"

5. Expect to encounter attacks of the enemy-on you, *and* those you pray for

6. Praise God In Advance For Victories

7. Don't Let The Outward Condition Of Those You Pray For, Make You Discouraged- Remember that your prayers are seeds and that they are undetectable for a while, before they begin to sprout up.

> "Learning to wait, and learning how to pray while we wait is challenging. It goes contrary to

---

[71] Alves, *Intercessors*, 70

our culture, which craves immediate gratification in worship and speed in results. Yet some of the greatest missionaries in the last few hundred years, people who have taken the gospel to places it had never been before, have waited long periods of time before ever seeing someone except Christ.
William Carey worked seven years before he led his first Hindu to the Lord in Burma. Adoniram Judson also served seven years before leading a soul to Christ cross culturally. It took 14 years of spreading the gospel in Western Africa before the first reported conversion… In Tahiti, 16 years… In New Zealand, nine. David Livingstone went through his entire missionary career in Zambia leading only one soul to Christ…"[72]

There is a story of a man who became a devout Christian and spent his life praying for the salvation of his seven sons. He became ill and after a while, he died, not having seen one of the boys saved. At the funeral the pastor ministered the word at the church and then they went to the grave site. The committal was done, the benediction given and the family and friends began to retreat to their cars. The oldest son however, asked his brothers to remain around the grave for a moment. Then he said to them, "Brothers, our father was a man of faith. He loved and served God with all of his heart, and yet, on his deathbed he was obviously having concerns. I believe he was fearful about dying. Now, if he was afraid to die with all of his faith and knowledge of God, what will happen to us if we die in our sins?" Then, right there, the miracle of answered prayer took place. Every one of the seven sons gave their lives to

---

[72] John Hull & Tim Elmore, *Pivotal Praying: Connecting with God in Times of Great Need* (Nashville: Thomas Nelson, 2002), p176,177

Jesus Christ. Their father never saw the seeds evolve on the earth, but he will experience a harvest in heaven. Don't quit praying! Whether you witness it here or not, you **ARE** making a difference.

Are You A Salvation Intercessor?

1. Do you have a burden to pray for lost souls on a regular basis?

2. When you are with a stranger, do you find yourself wanting to know if that person is saved? Are you burdened to pray until he/she is? [73]

---

[73] Alves, *Intercessor,* 72

Chapter 12 Mercy and Grace Intercessor

The English poet William Blake said, "Where Mercy, love, and pity dwell there God is dwelling too."[74] One of the valuable areas of intercession is that of "Mercy" intercession. Mercy intercessors may be the most tolerant of all intercessors. On one hand, they live to release others from having to pay the penalty of sin. On the other hand, they are begging God to heal, deliver, and provide breakthroughs for people who have been labeled: "lost"; "loser"; "loco"; "licentious"; "lewd"; "labor-allergic" ; or just a plain louse.

A. Lost-people who are unable to find their way to God that purpose without help

B. Loser-people who have a history of failure

C. Loco-a slang term for foolish, crazy acting

D. Licentious -people lacking moral discipline especially sexually

E. Lewd-people preoccupied with moral looseness-addicted to it

---

[74]William Blake (1757-1827), British poet, painter, mystic. From SONGS OF INNOCENCE. The Divine Image (l. 17-20). . . The Complete Poems [William Blake]. Alicia Ostriker, ed. (1977) Penguin Books.

F. Labor-allergic-people who are lazy, won't work and because of that, poverty has found

G. Louse-people with nasty, unethical character who have little regard for others

The Mercy intercessor has to have a heart... for everyone. While the most vile sinner, killer, brutal murderer, sex offender, is being taken to the hill to be crucified, the death chamber to be electrocuted, or sentenced to be "buried beneath the jail/prison", the Mercy intercessor is crying out to God for his/her life. They are never in the crowd crying "crucify him", "stone her."

"Your Grace and Mercy Brought Me Through"

Mercy is defined as "leniency and compassion shown towards offenders by a person or agency charged with administering justice."[75] As children of God, we have the capacity to judge on the behalf of the kingdom of God. Our tongues are "ready writers." Elijah said to King Ahab that it would not rain again accept by his (Elijah's) word. In other words, he knew the power he possessed as a Dominion carrier (tapped into God... Alone). The blessing of the land was in his mouth.

Grace is defined as "a disposition to kindness and compassion; it is making something more attractive by adding something to it; free and unmerited favor or beneficence of God."

If the truth be told, all of us must agree with the songwriter, "Your grace and mercy brought me through. I'm living this moment because of you"[76] (well, I know it's true

---

[75] http://www.thefreedictionary.com/grace,Accessed June 17,2013

about me if nobody else is willing to admit it) "Somebody prayed for me", is evident in every area of my life. What about yours?

The concept of the Mercy intercessor is not new, but coupling it with "grace" is. It is possible for a person to experience *mercy*, without experiencing grace. Mercy is an act of forgiveness, but Grace adds to it a gift in spite of the offense.

An Act Of Mercy

When I was a youth I played and loved the game of baseball as much as I did eating and sleeping. My father, on the other hand, loved me more than he loved to see me play. He had a strict set of rules, a standard set for our home. It was very simple and it carried a penalty with it. Go to school, pay attention, stay out of trouble and focus on getting good grades. The consequences of breaking those standards were painful (in more ways than one). one of those was that baseball would become a spectator, not a participant sport. Well, I tried to test the standard and found the punishment waiting for me. To my surprise however, halfway through the summer, after watching my tears and sadness, as I stood in the window peering out at my teammates going to practice after practice, game after the game, he allowed me to rejoin the team. That was an act of mercy. I absolutely did not deserve to play. I knew the consequences and still violated the rules. He could have let the punishment meet the crime, but instead, he showed mercy. He showed compassion, leniency towards me. His love for me, was greater than my love and respect for him.

Mercy is birthed to reveal the love of the Father to His children, despite their foolish hearts, in hopes that they will turn towards Him. You do remember time and time again as

---

[76] Frank D. Williams, Your Grace and Mercy Brought Me Through, http://www.hymnary.org/text/your_grace_and_mercy_brought_me_through

the children of Israel were out on their journey to the promised land, making foolish decisions to rebel, complain and become "rearview mirror" lookers, that Moses pleaded for mercy on their behalf, so God would not destroy them, don't you?

Mercy Turns To Grace

Jesus prayed to the Father to forgive the lying, the conspiracy, the wounding, the mockery and disbelief, as He took His place on the cross. That was an act of mercy as well. However, when he died for their (and our) sins and offered eternity with Him to a world that rejected Him, THAT is Grace. A gift, in spite of our sinful actions? A gift that should by all stretches of the imagination be given to those who love Him and were faithful to Him without failure.

Mercy and grace intercessors keep certain scriptures close to their hearts, so that they never forget to pray.

> Ephesians 2:8- "For by grace you have been saved through faith; and that not of yourselves, *it is* the gift of God";
>
> Luke 6:28- "Bless those who curse you, pray for those who mistreat you".
>
> Matthew 5:44- "But I say to you, love your enemies and pray for those who persecute you,
>
> Genesis 12:3 - "And I will bless those who bless you, And the one who curses you I will curse. And in you all the families of the earth will be blessed."

The Mercy and Grace intercessor understands the Favor of God on the life of the true believer and exercises restraint in their prayers. They are much different than David, who was obviously a warfare intercessor.

Psalm 35:4 - "Let those be ashamed and dishonored who seek my life; Let those be turned back and humiliated who devise evil against me."

Psalm 54:3-5 - For strangers have risen against me And violent men have sought my life; They have not set God before them. Selah. ⁴ Behold, God is my helper; The Lord is the sustainer of my soul. ⁵ He will recompense the evil to my foes; Destroy them in Your faithfulness.

Bearing a Cost for the Undeserved

"Mercy intercessors; however are the good neighbors of prayer, who travel highways of the hurting, looking for someone to lift up. They are God's living stethoscopes. They do not regard the outward appearance, but instead hear the root of a person's pain in order to extend the Mercy of God to that root. When lined up with their anointing, mercy intercessors are is able to weep for their enemies as they are for their friends because they have a "cross"-eye view of God's creation."[77]

The mercy and grace intercessor is always common even to the dismay of many, leaning on the side of forgiveness as opposed to judgment. They never forget their own salvation experience. They know that Jesus will cross for them when they were undeserving. "While we were yet sinners, Christ died for the ungodly."[78] I don't know about you, but I think *that* deserved a praise break. Okay, are you done? Then let's go on, but you cannot, EVER forget that.

---

[77] Alves, *Intercessor*, 108,109

[78] Romans 5:8 KVJ

It is for sure that mercy and grace intercessors always keep at least five things at heart:

1. They love unconditionally, "It is the cross I bear, and it hurts sometimes".

2. They do not keep records of wrong. Wrong is a reason to help not harm. It is a teaching moment

3. They know "hurt people, hurt people"

4. They believe delivered and healed people, deliver and heal people

5. They will fight to the finish, holding on to the "7 times 70" forgiveness plan of Jesus

Unconditional Lovers

The rarest of breeds of all humanity are those who exercise unconditional love. Yes, I know people claim to have it. Everyone knows it is a good idea to have it, but the truth is, it is undoubtedly a quest most have not attained. The Mercy intercessor is in this rare breed category. Unconditional lovers are often criticized for defending (in prayer), those who may be called offenders/perpetrators. And yet, is this not the posture of Jesus, when he stands as an intercessor for us? No crime is too great for Him to turn His back on us. No act is so vile that He would refuse to offer us love. The blood He shared had no conditions on it. It simply spelled out for all of us to see, I LOVE YOU! The mercy and grace intercessor walks in the same shoes, much to the dismay of people who would rather see the extent of the penalty for breaking the law given to those who have fallen (unless of course it is them or someone close to them).

Your Record Is Expunged

There is a difference between a pardon and an expungement. A pardon does not erase the event. The person is granted "executive clemency." It says that someone in power has forgiven you of a crime you committed. In the world, presidents and state governors have a right to do this.

When an expungement is granted, the incident in question disappears. It is treated as it never occurred. Only a judge can grant that. When any of us have broken the law and have our records marred and lives stained with the label "felon" (too often till death), we are at the mercy of a man or woman, who lives in flesh, to decide cleansing or not. Thank God that is in the natural only.

In the spiritual, which rules beyond the natural, God is our great judge. He sent Jesus to die for our sins. God prepared a body for His Spirit, took on the flesh of His creation and called Himself Jesus. We know Him as the "Son" of God. His life and blood was given to EXPUNGE our sinful, fallen life. We Are in essence born again into the "Genesis One" Pattern. There Is a Restoration of "Imago Dei" (the image of God).

Mercy and grace intercessors see people as recipients of what they themselves as intercessors, are called (mercy and grace). Thereby, they see everyone in their "hidden in Christ" state (or at least potentially). In other words their hope is in the salvation of the perpetrator so they can personally experience, what they have been positionally given.

Hurt People Hurt People

Mercy and grace intercessors have to be students of hurting people. The mercy and grace intercessors are always digging. They have a great need to discover the root of people's pains always hoping and praying to get them healed. The expression "hurt people, hurt people" is not a new one. Dr. Sandra Wilson has written a book on the subject and explains that lies, denial, abuse are some of the many causes of the hurt seen in people. From her personal experiences she writes about how abuse passes to generations. That abuse may be sexual, substance, physical or psychological (emotional).

Hurt people usually begin their abuse with themselves. Their anger about what has been done to them, is also a sense of shame, that often causes a shut down and a secret passion for releasing their shame, anger and confusion on another. This is often done on someone as weak as they were when they were hurt, or at least weaker than they are presently. "Someone has to pay for my pain", is their motto.

The mercy and grace intercessor sees beyond their cruelty or crime and sees the bitterness, depression, escapism, fears, and low self worth. They respond to the NEED of the offender not the DEED.

Have you ever heard the story of the person who asked the mother which one of her children did she love the most? The mother responded, "The one that needs me the most." That my dear friend, is the heart of Jesus, who is the ultimate mercy and grace intercessor. You hear him reminding each of us daily, "It is not those who are healthy who need a physician, but those who are sick ... (Mark 2:17 NASB)

If We Can Just Get You Delivered...

The mercy and grace intercessor knows well the scriptural references where Jesus and others set free people who were bound, and what happened as a result. Make no doubt about it, this is not an airtight argument, but is generally true with grateful people.

- The woman at the well in John 4 was set free from too much for us to expound upon fully here, but here are a few: cultural distancing; pride; low self-esteem; social outcast

- The man who made his home in a graveyard was set free from unknown trauma/emotional issues he had him cutting himself with stones (Mark 5)
- The tax collector Matthew, called away by Jesus, from his old life as a thief to his community, decided to invite all of his former colleagues to his house to meet the one who changed his life (Luke 5:27- 29)
- Zacchaeus, also a tax collector, hated by his community as a trader, gets set free from his old life as Jesus invites Himself to visit the collector's home. Zacchaeus responds by saying "Behold, Lord, half of my possessions I will give to the poor, and if I have defrauded anyone of anything, I will give back four times as much." (Luke 19:8)
- Paul, after his experience on the Damascus Road, never forgot his conversion. He alluded to this in every letter he wrote, calling himself a slave/servant of Christ. His past he labeled as dung; forgotten.
- Peter reaches down to pick up a man who was crippled for eight years and bedridden. His healing changed his outlook. We know that because he went to two cities and got them saved. (Acts 9:32-35)

All of these stories are about broken people who experience the love of God and show themselves as grateful recipients of his mercy and grace, therefore they responded by doing something for him in the lives of others. Why, because what is sown in your life for good, you ought to be sowing in the lives of others.

Fight to the Finish

Mercy and grace intercessors have, as we mentioned earlier, a "cross" mentality. They do not believe in giving up. Their rest and reward comes when the warfare is over. Then, they see the result of their prayer seeds and say, "It is finished."

> There is a great story about a man who was sleeping at night in his cabin when suddenly his room is filled with light and the Savior appeared. The Lord told the man he had work for him to do, and showed him a large rock in front of his cabin. The Lord explained that the man was to push against the rock with all his might. This the man did, day after day. For many years he toiled from sun up to sun down, his shoulders set squarely against the cold massive surface of the unmoving rock, pushing with all his might. Each night the man returned to his cabin sore and worn out, feeling that his whole day had been spent in vain.
>
> Seeing that the man was showing signs of discouragement, the adversary decided to enter the picture by placing thoughts into the man's weary mind: "you have been pushing against that rock for a long time and it hasn't budged", he said. "Why kill yourself over this? You are never going to move it." This gave the man the impression that the task was impossible and that he was a failure. These thoughts discouraged the man. He thought to himself, "Why kill myself over this?" "I'll keep put in my time but from now on I will be giving just the minimum effort and that will be good enough." He had made up his mind, it was settled, and then he decided to make this a matter of prayer. He took it to the Lord, and he said, "Lord, I have labored long and hard in your service, giving all my strength

to do what you asked me to do. Yet, in all of the time, I have not even budged the rock by a half a millimeter. What's wrong? Why am I failing?" The Lord responded compassionately, "My child, when I asked you to serve me and you accepted, I told you that your task was to push against the rock with all your strength, which you have done. Never once did I mention to you that I expected you to move it. Your task was to push. And now you come to me, with your strength spent, thinking that you have failed. But, is that really so? Look at yourself. Your arms are strong and muscled, your back sinew and brown, your hands are calloused from constant pressure, and your legs have become massive and hard. Through opposition you have grown much and your abilities now surpass that which you used to have. Yet you haven't moved the rock. But your calling was to be obedient and to push and to exercise your faith and trust in My wisdom. This you have done. I, my friend, will now move the rock."

At times, when we hear a word from God, we tend to use our own intellect to decipher what He wants from or for us, when actually what God wants is just simple obedience and faith in Him.

The Weapon of Weeping

It has more than once been stated, that there are times when God asks nothing of His children except silence, patience and tears. At other times, tears are the introduction to and motivation, for a plan to transform a nation or resurrect something or someone that has died. Such was the case for Nehemiah and Jesus.

Nehemiah is recorded as having wept at the news of the destruction of his hometown. The people were scattered, and confusion and the land was in ruins. Weeping is an act of sorrow. But, it is also an act of healing and welling up of confidence and strength; motivation to do something about the condition at hand.

Jesus saw the faith of his friends Mary and Martha, and the condition of his friend Lazarus, then he wept. As He wept he raised him from the dead. He also wept over Jerusalem (Luke 19:41-44), because they were blind to salvation and being held captive by religious leaders. Are you weeping over your city? Are you moved by its famine, failures, fractured relationships, fallen morals and leaders? Is your weeping followed by a plan to pray, to penetrate the darkness, to transform the terrain, to resurrect the dead?

Four-fold Sign of Tears

1. They signal heaven that we surrender and need help
   You cannot do everything on your own. Angels are standing by waiting for an assignment. You are on their radar. Let them help you.

2. They identify the crier as a person of compassion/care/concern. The place of tears says to God, this person can be trusted to hold precious cargo for those for whom they are weeping, to help them get free.

3. They Cleanse the Callousness- they break up cold, hard places in the lives of the ones crying and also can be contagious for people who are watching them cry. Tears are infectious. One person can begin crying and affect a whole room of people; changing the atmosphere and moving ordinary people *and* sympathetic people to do extraordinary things, together.

4. They Soak the Soul- tears are a cleanser; a refresher medication, that brings us into the life of others, vicariously carrying their issues. They make us one with others. They fill us with a righteous calling, that ignites us beyond selfish ambition, refusing to settle for a life that is all about "ME."

A Tear List To Jumpstart You

Abortion Clinics

Broken homes

Child Abuse
Drugs abuse and result

Education Cost

Fatherlessnes

Gang violence

Homelessness

Incarceration

Juvenile delinquency

Kingdom of God (lost in the desire to please the world and be like it)

Legislation of immorality by our politicians

Money becoming God

Networking (social) that has the appearance of building "friendships", but are mirages

Obesity in America

Poverty

Quiet time with God...we can't be alone with him because of our addiction to technology

Racism

Sexuality crises

Trafficking of Humans

Uncommon weather patterns

Veterans who are coming home from war and in need of serious counseling and therapy

World and Civil terrorism

A Word of Caution

Because these areas cause one to weep so for others; there must be a constant guard against depression, becoming a hermit; hiding away; angry that God has failed; or is too slow in His responses. Endurance is key. The mercy and grace intercessor needs mental, emotional and physical outlets. They need time and places to breathe, to laugh, to play. Like every intercessor, you need a journal and personal time in the Word of God. Carrying for the world and not your personal soul can eventually be unhealthy. Keep watch over your soul as well. Sometimes doctors are the worst patients.

Portrait of a Modern Day Mercy and Grace Intercessor

Let me close this chapter with a powerful story about one of life's heroes.

> "In his outstanding biography *Teresa of the Poor,* Renzo Allegri shares his interviews with Mother Teresa-a woman who saw Jesus as her husband and all the hurting people of this world as their children. She believed her role was to care for her Spouse's children by praying, living and serving among the poor. Allegri says, 'It did not matter to her that the person was a, saint or a criminal, an athlete or a leper, a person in power or a person in despair. To her, that person was a child of God for whose eternal salvation Jesus died on the cross."[79]

Beloved, may your name be written with hers and all of heavens heroes, as you tirelessly pursue the calling to be a mercy and grace intercessor. Indeed, you are a special breed. It's been an honor to serve you.

---

[79] Alves, *Intercessor,* 109,110

Chapter 13 The Crisis Intercessor

It began as a bright winter day, December 10th, one indelibly imprinted in my mind. There was a knock on the door. Who could it be? I was not expecting anyone. A couple of hours earlier I had just received a call from my dad that my mother had taken ill and I should come home to see her. In the midst of gathering some things together, the knock at the door turned the already becoming cloudy day, into one of pitch darkness. Two of the members of the church I pastored were standing there with tear filled eyes. Their next words sent my life and my family's (dad, brother and sister) into a downward spiral. They said, "Mae Nell didn't make it." This is almost 30 years later and although time in prayer has erased the wounds of that time, the scars remind me of the crisis. The life of my father, brother and sister, as well as mine, would go through a time of unprepared for, emotional and physical changes, that would take years to correct. At 49 years of age, my mother was gone. I had not thought about it, neither had any of us, but she was the master-link in the family chain. Crisis was undoubtedly upon us and we had not a real clue how to handle it!

What do you do when crisis arises in your home? What about in your city? Nation? Have you ever been passing by an accident and instead of being a "rubber neck" driver (as so many are), holding up traffic, you begin to pray for the person, family, rescuers? Do you find yourself calmest at "crunch" time, saying to yourself, "I am here at this moment, when things are at their worst, because God wanted someone who could handle it to be present? If so, then you are definitely reading the right chapter.

What Constitutes A Crisis?

Anything that presents an obstacle, threat or trauma can or may be categorized as a crisis. They are things that take place that put our life at a standstill and present opportunity to derail our purpose in life, destroying our sense of peace and direction. It also has at its foundation, the ability to distance us from our relationship with God.

Years ago, a member of our church experienced the tragic death of her mother, who was severely burned in a fire at her home. The daughter made it clear that she could never return to the church and look at the place where her mother used to sit.

Wikipedia defines crisis as, "Any event that is, or expected to lead to, an unstable and dangerous situation affecting an individual, group, community or whole society. Crises are deemed to be negative changes in the security, economic, political, societal, or environmental affairs, especially when they occur abruptly with little or no warning."[80]

Crisis can be categorized in four areas: personal; family (which personal also effects); community; and national, or world. They are unexpected events that surface, throwing our equilibrium off. They throw us off of our emotional and spiritual balance. They cause us to pause and wonder where to turn and who to turn to. They threaten our dreams or goals. Every time they arise, we are faced with the task of discovering what is in us. Do we have the fortitude to overcome whatever it is.

John Hall, in his book on *Pivotal Praying*, says that crisis care is actually a normal part of ministers' work. He quotes a pastor from Evanston Illinois: "The church is always in crisis mode. A new convert throws her live in boyfriend out of the house, and now she has to make up the difference in

---

[80] http://en.wikipedia.org/wiki/Crisis,Accessed June 17,2013

rent. You get word that a junior high Sunday school teachers telling her class that, without glossolalia (speaking in tongues) they're second-rate Christians. A van load of youth are injured on the way to church camp. The local plant closes and three of your deacons are out of work. A staff member quits in a flurry of recrimination. A prominent church member shows up on the DUI list of the local paper. A business meeting ignites over item 3.B in the church budget. And that's just this week."[81]

The First Recorded Crisis

It may be a surprise to you, but if we accept the definition offered earlier for crisis, then we have to agree that the first crisis is found in Genesis 3 in Scripture. It was the story of personal, family, community and national crisis, at the same time.

Adam ignores his wife Eve while she is being given attention to by the serpent. One may not see this as a crisis, and yet it is an event that, as the definition says, "led to an unstable and dangerous situation affecting an individual, group, community and whole society (future as well)." Adam's negligence and Eve's choices gave to the enemy of heaven, "dominion on the earth." They began a war that exists to this day. Great turmoil, tragedy, grief, sorrow and shame have come out of their actions.

Every decision you and I make has the potential to bring one of two choices: fruit or fatality; blessings or curses; rejoicing in honor or sorrow in crisis. You may hear this from me often, which means it is vitally significant, "We should never take lightly the power of a "seed." Note well, that our actions, every one of them, are seeds.

Personal

---

[81] Hull, *Pivotal* Praying, 18

Adam's ignoring of Eve causes her to pay attention to a voice outside of the Word and Will of God. This will bring division in a marriage. It resulted in Eve having to experience the pains of childbirth (which she was obviously not originally designed to have to go through). In other words, the producing of the *seed* planted, would have to be paid for by the harvest of great labor pains.

Family

The decisions in the Garden of Eden open the door for enemy spirits to dominate in the earth. the loss of those spirits are numerous, but come from the same source. Here are a list of a few: the spirit of pride; the spirit of jealousy; the spirit of anger; the spirit of death (by murder); the spirit of competition (that began it all with the sons); and the spirit of rejection.

One son, who is the offspring of a father who didn't pay attention to his assignment, his jealousy, and rejecting the counsel of God, allowed himself to kill his own brother. Talking about family crisis? That definitely ranks high!

Community

Cain, now excommunicated from his immediate family has to find his own way. By the way, he experiences, as did his parents, the core of where the word poverty comes from: The absence of God. True poverty, which is a crisis condition, is not merely the absence of money. It is the absence of God. You see, if you have God, you have provision. Money or resources can be accessed, again. True poverty then becomes the inability to reproduce fruit, because of barrenness that is caused by sins. Fret not however, all lack of resources is not because of sin. some lack is temporary with purpose. You may be experiencing it because God is using you as a test for testimony (which means your barrenness will be lifted in *Kairos*-God time).

Take note this, where Cain went, nobody could kill him. He had to live in the misery of his decision, dismissed from the presence of God and family. He was in essence, "imprisoned." He was definitely experiencing "true poverty." Is that a crisis? You bet it is! Whatever gifts he had, and could share, had to be lived without, because of *his* decisions.

National/World

Adam and Eve's decision did not ***just*** bring crisis to their family, it affected the world. Sin entered the world and has caused many to die without knowing, experiencing and enjoying the love of God in Christ Jesus.

Watchmen Anointing/Night Watchmen

While we will not fully go into all that this anointing entails, suffice it to say that all believers are in a sense, called to be "watchmen." As a crisis intercessor you are called by God to be "night watchmen". In other words, watch over our world and the "night" seasons, or times of trial.

The crisis intercessor *looks* for trouble so they can pray. They are the "*storm chasers*" of prayer. They are constant news watchers. The crisis intercessor checks news flashes (even around the world) as often as possible, to see what things are affecting the lives of others. They are on call day and night. They work in the "Spiritual Emergency Room" of intercession. They do not fear casualties, they run to them.

Fearless In the Face of Catastrophe

Crisis intercessors are the team that begins praying, instead of shouting "Oh my God, what are we going to do?" They believe that our God should be magnified, made bigger, over every catastrophe. They understand that the situation is critical or life-threatening and make a decision ***not*** to panic, but to pray. I mean, really, if it's bigger than you can handle, why *not* turn it over to somebody GREATER!

Ever met people who were just always ready for a fight? Well, that's you, really! Crisis intercessors live with an "edge" on them. "Oh, is that what you have?" David exhibited crisis intercession when he went to bring the food to his brothers while they were in the war against the Philistines. The army of the Lord had "*cowered*" them before the giant Goliath, shaming the name of God before every people group who would hear the story. Their reputation was at stake. Here is the dreadful scene: a war that couldn't be avoided; a giant postured before them; defeat looks like its awaiting them; and the name of the Lord is being trashed and trampled upon. David comes on the scene, an unlikely intercessor, fearless in posture, saying, "What shall be done to the man that killeth this Philistine, and taketh away the reproach from Israel? For who is this uncircumcised Philistine, that he should defy the armies of the living God?" (I Samuel 17:26 K JV) that my friend is the courage, confidence and demeanor of a crisis intercessor.

The Warfare Family

Crisis intercessors are really a part of the warfare intercessors family. Whenever any crisis arrives, these two teams partner together to form a hedge around the perimeter and to stand toe to toe with the enemy, battling until victory or breakthrough comes forth. Knowing that, you have to expect "attack that will distract." Listen to what Elizabeth Alves writes, "Satan doesn't fight fair in this battle. If he can keep you from praying, he will assail you with doubt, discouragement and fear as you look at seemingly impossible circumstances. This deceiver will try to make you feel you are being objective and getting a lay of the land as you look at the situation. In reality his goal is to sideline you with an attitude of hopelessness and passivity."[82]

Satan will do anything he can to cause personal issues to distract you from interceding for national calamities. He uses tools like: "You're too busy"; "You have your own problems"; "This can wait, Can't it?" The crisis intercessor learns to ignore the voice and priority setting of the enemy. He will always attempt to set priorities for you. Remember who orders your day. The crisis intercessor understands, "we do not take orders or even advice, from the adversary." Deceit is always a part of his motive.

As Long As The Earth Remains... Seed Time and Harvest

There are always two kinds of seeds planted in the earth: seeds of divinity and seeds of destruction. And John 10:10, Jesus said, "the thief comes only to steal, kill and destroy; I have come that they may have life, and have it to the full." The assignment of the thief is to sow destructive, deadly seeds, expecting to reap a harvest that will steal life, the very breath, from man. Every storm, every tragedy, every family crisis is meant to cause division, devastation and destiny distraction. The crisis intercessor has to stand with Jesus, believing that his/her prayers are seeds of life for those who are in desperation. Crisis intercessors are spiritual CPR givers, life resuscitators. They provide the electrical current that gets the failing heart back on its natural/spiritual, rhythm.

There's A Storm Out Over The Ocean

A Pentecostal song that I like says, "there's a storm out over life's ocean and it's moving, this old way. If your souls not, anchored in Jesus, you will surely, drift away."[83] I mentioned this earlier, that the crisis intercessor has a

---

[82] Alves, *Becoming A Prayer Warrior*, 105

[83] Public domain

responsibility of fighting storms. They do not wait for crisis or storms to arrive. If they see a storm coming, they ward it off. In other words the crisis intercessor is also a crisis "prevention" warrior.

Lord Possess Me

Author James Goll writes about his visit to Wales to see Samuel Howells, the son of the famous Welsh intercessor Rees Howells, who founded the Bible College of Wales at Swansea. He sat before him and asked over and over about how to redo the wells of crisis intercession. He said, "I had one burning question, and I kept asking it." "How is it that your father got this level of revelation and authority for crisis intercession?" Goll finally got his answer when his friend got down on her knees and crawled over in front of Howells chair and said, "Mr. Howell, you must understand. Our nation is in crisis. The world is in crisis. And we need authority in prayer that your father and those who prayed with him had..."[84] This my dear friend, was Samuel Howells response, that would impact James Goll's life forever, and has mine as well, since reading it: "The Lord's servant was *possessed* by God."[85] That should be the prayer of EVERY intercessor, but especially the crisis intercessor. "Lord *Possess* Me!" "Lord *Consume* Me!" Take Over! My time, talents, treasure, mind, body, all of me belongs to You!

Biblical examples

Personal-Hannah

---

[84] James W. Goll, *Prayer Storm: the Hour That Changes the World* (Shippensburg, PA: Destiny Image, 2008), 90

[85] Ibid., 90

I Samuel 1:1-8

1 There was a certain man from Ramathaim, a Zuphite from the hill country of Ephraim, whose name was Elkanah son of Jeroham, the son of Elihu, the son of Tohu, the son of Zuph, an Ephraimite. ² He had two wives; one was called Hannah and the other Peninnah. Peninnah had children, but Hannah had none.

³ Year after year this man went up from his town to worship and sacrifice to the LORD Almighty at Shiloh, where Hophni and Phinehas, the two sons of Eli, were priests of the LORD. ⁴ Whenever the day came for Elkanah to sacrifice, he would give portions of the meat to his wife Peninnah and to all her sons and daughters. ⁵ But to Hannah he gave a double portion because he loved her, and the LORD had closed her womb. ⁶ Because the LORD had closed Hannah's womb, her rival kept provoking her in order to irritate her. ⁷ This went on year after year. Whenever Hannah went up to the house of the LORD, her rival provoked her till she wept and would not eat. ⁸ Her husband Elkanah would say to her, "Hannah, why are you weeping? Why don't you eat? Why are you downhearted? Don't I mean more to you than ten sons?"

Family-Abraham

Genesis 18:16-26

¹⁶ When the men got up to leave, they looked down toward Sodom, and Abraham walked along with them to see them on their way. ¹⁷ Then the LORD said, "Shall I hide from Abraham what I am about to do? ¹⁸ Abraham will surely become a great and powerful nation, and all nations on earth will be blessed through him. ¹⁹ For I have chosen him, so that he will direct his children and his household after him to keep the way of the LORD by doing what is right and just, so that the LORD will bring about for Abraham what he has promised him."

²⁰ Then the LORD said, "The outcry against Sodom and Gomorrah is so great and their sin so grievous ²¹ that I will go down and see if what they have done is as bad as the outcry that has reached me. If not, I will know."

²² The men turned away and went toward Sodom, but Abraham remained standing before the LORD.²³ Then Abraham approached him and said: "Will you sweep away the righteous with the wicked? ²⁴ What if there are fifty righteous people in the city? Will you really sweep it away and not spare the place for the sake of the fifty righteous people in it? ²⁵ Far be it from you to do such a thing—to kill the righteous with the wicked, treating the righteous and the wicked alike. Far be it from you! Will not the Judge of all the earth do right?"

²⁶ The LORD said, "If I find fifty righteous people in the city of Sodom, I will spare the whole place for their sake." (Abraham was interceding for Sodom because his nephew and nephew's family lived in that city)

Leader-Rhoda

Acts 12:1-5

¹It was about this time that King Herod arrested some who belonged to the church, intending to persecute them. ²He had James, the brother of John, put to death with the sword. ³When he saw that this met with approval among the Jews, he proceeded to seize Peter also. This happened during the Festival of Unleavened Bread. ⁴After arresting him, he put him in prison, handing him over to be guarded by four squads of four soldiers each. Herod intended to bring him out for public trial after the Passover.

⁵So Peter was kept in prison, but the church was earnestly praying to God for him.

Community-Extended Family-Jesus

Mark 4:35-41

³⁵That day when evening came, he said to his disciples, "Let us go over to the other side." ³⁶Leaving the crowd behind, they took him along, just as he was, in the boat. There were also other boats with him. ³⁷A furious squall came up, and the waves broke over the boat, so that it was nearly swamped. ³⁸Jesus was in the stern, sleeping on a cushion. The disciples woke him and said to him, "Teacher, don't you care if we drown?"

³⁹He got up, rebuked the wind and said to the waves, "Quiet! Be still!" Then the wind died down and it was completely calm.

⁴⁰He said to his disciples, "Why are you so afraid? Do you still have no faith?"

⁴¹ They were terrified and asked each other, "Who is this? Even the wind and the waves obey him!"

Nation-Esther, Ezekiel, Nehemiah

Esther 5

When Mordecai learned all that had been done, he tore his clothes, put on sackcloth and ashes, and went out into the midst of the city and wailed loudly and bitterly. ² He went as far as the king's gate, for no one was to enter the king's gate clothed in sackcloth. ³ In each and every province where the command and decree of the king came, there was great mourning among the Jews, with fasting, weeping and wailing; and many lay on sackcloth and ashes.
⁴ Then Esther's maidens and her eunuchs came and told her, and the queen writhed in great anguish. And she sent garments to clothe Mordecai that he might remove his sackcloth from him, but he did not accept *them*. ⁵ Then Esther summoned Hathach from the king's eunuchs, whom the king had appointed to attend her, and ordered him *to go* to Mordecai to learn what this *was* and why it *was*. ⁶ So Hathach went out to Mordecai to the city square in front of the king's gate. ⁷ Mordecai told him all that had happened to him, and the exact amount of money that Haman had promised to pay to the king's treasuries for the destruction of the Jews. ⁸ He also gave him a copy of the text of the edict which had been issued in Susa for their destruction, that he might show Esther and inform her, and to order her to go in to the king

to implore his favor and to plead with him for her people. ⁹ Hathach came back and related Mordecai's words to Esther. ¹⁰ Then Esther spoke to Hathach and ordered him *to reply* to Mordecai: ¹¹ "All the king's servants and the people of the king's provinces know that for any man or woman who comes to the king to the inner court who is not summoned, he has but one law, that he be put to death, unless the king holds out to him the golden scepter so that he may live. And I have not been summoned to come to the king for these thirty days." ¹² They related Esther's words to Mordecai.

¹³ Then Mordecai told *them* to reply to Esther, "Do not imagine that you in the king's palace can escape any more than all the Jews. ¹⁴ For if you remain silent at this time, relief and deliverance will arise for the Jews from another place and you and your father's house will perish. And who knows whether you have not attained royalty for such a time as this?"

¹⁵ Then Esther told *them* to reply to Mordecai, ¹⁶ "Go, assemble all the Jews who are found in Susa, and fast for me; do not eat or drink for three days, night or day. I and my maidens also will fast in the same way. And thus I will go in to the king, which is not according to the law; and if I perish, I perish." ¹⁷ So Mordecai went away and did just as Esther had commanded him.

Ezekiel 37:1-10

The hand of the LORD was on me, and he brought me out by the Spirit of the LORD and set me in the middle of a valley; it was full of bones. ² He led me back and forth among them, and I saw a great many bones on the floor of the valley, bones that were very dry. ³ He asked me, "Son of man, can these bones live?"

I said, "Sovereign LORD, you alone know."

⁴ Then he said to me, "Prophesy to these bones and say to them, 'Dry bones, hear the word of the LORD! ⁵ This is what the Sovereign LORD says to these bones: I will make breath[a] enter you, and you will come to life. ⁶ I will attach tendons to you and make flesh come upon you and cover you with skin; I will put breath in you, and you will come to life. Then you will know that I am the LORD.'"

⁷ So I prophesied as I was commanded. And as I was prophesying, there was a noise, a rattling sound, and the bones came together, bone to bone. ⁸ I looked, and tendons and flesh appeared on them and skin covered them, but there was no breath in them.

⁹ Then he said to me, "Prophesy to the breath; prophesy, son of man, and say to it, 'This is what the Sovereign LORD says: Come, breath, from the four winds and breathe into these slain, that they may live.'" ¹⁰ So I prophesied as he commanded me, and breath entered them; they came to life and stood up on their feet—a vast army.

Nehemiah 1

The words of Nehemiah son of Hakaliah:

In the month of Kislev in the twentieth year, while I was in the citadel of Susa, ² Hanani, one of my brothers, came from Judah with some other men, and I questioned them about the Jewish remnant that had survived the exile, and also about Jerusalem.

³ They said to me, "Those who survived the exile and are back in the province are in great trouble and disgrace. The wall of Jerusalem is broken down, and its gates have been burned with fire."

⁴ When I heard these things, I sat down and wept. For some days I mourned and fasted and prayed before the God of heaven. ⁵ Then I said:

"LORD, the God of heaven, the great and awesome God, who keeps his covenant of love with those who love him and keep his commandments, ⁶ let your ear be attentive and your eyes open to hear the prayer your servant is praying before you day and night for your servants, the people of Israel. I confess the sins we Israelites, including myself and my father's family, have committed against you. ⁷ We have acted very wickedly toward you. We have not obeyed the commands, decrees and laws you gave your servant Moses.

⁸ "Remember the instruction you gave your servant Moses, saying, 'If you are unfaithful, I will scatter you among the nations, ⁹ but if you return to me and obey my commands, then even if your exiled people are at the farthest horizon, I will gather them from there and bring them to the place I have chosen as a dwelling for my Name.'

¹⁰ "They are your servants and your people, whom you redeemed by your great strength and your mighty hand. ¹¹ Lord, let your ear be attentive to the prayer of this your servant and to the prayer of your servants who delight in revering your name. Give your servant success today by granting him favor in the presence of this man."

I was cupbearer to the king.

World-Jesus

Luke 23:34(a) - Jesus said, "Father, forgive them, for they do not know what they are doing."

Modern Day Crisis Issues

War

Gun Violence

Abortion (National statistics - 1200 of the 4000 babies that die daily are African American...in other words...33% of all abortions are from African American women. This is from a population which is only 13.6%)

Obesity-especially childhood

Economic, America in debt

Politics has become the new religion of our day

Terrorism continuing to rise (especially in America)

Homosexuality/same-sex marriage legislated by our politicians

Dennis Kimbo, writes a chapter called, *The Greatest Need of Man: Prayer*, in his book, *What Makes The Great, Great.* He says of prayer; "When millions are troubled, uncertain and confused, this need takes on a new and vital importance. There has never been a time when our brothers and sisters were more desperately in need of faith, hope, courage, peace of mind -of standards and ideals by which to live. There's never been a time or moment during the course of history when humanity didn't need something to cling to, something on which to build, something enduring an everlasting; something to secure us to the floor as we face the stiff winds of change; something that will provide firm structure in fragile lives."[86]

He made that statement 15 years ago. If it was so then, it is even more so today. Twenty years from now when people are reading this book, they will say the same thing. Times have become even more turbulent and society has relaxed almost every moral standard. It is high time for crisis intercessors to cry out to "El Shaddai." One of the meanings of "El Shaddai," is that he is the Almighty God who can take a wind that is blowing against you, and reverse it to blow in your favor. Prophesy to the Wind Intercessors! Do it Now!

Shifting The Atmosphere: No Death, On My Watch

While others often accept the natural consequences of things and answers provided by experts, crisis intercessors are often moved by God to change things. Dutch sheets records this story in his book; *The Beginner's Guide to Intercessory Prayer,* "During heart surgery, a young wife and mother died on the operating table. She was finally resuscitated, but never regained her consciousness. The doctors asserted that this was for the best, as her brain had been deprived of oxygen and would never again function properly. The pastor and others comforted her husband and prayed with him.

---

[86] Dennis Kimbro, *What Makes the Great Great*, Reprint ed. (New York: Broadway Books, 1998), *257*

Three nights later the pastor awakened, realized his wife was not in bed, and went to look for her. He found her lying on the living room floor, groaning. When he asked her what was wrong, she said, she didn't know, she didn't understand it, but she couldn't let the young woman die. For the next three nights, she lay on the floor, groaning and praying all night long.

On the following day, the woman in the hospital suddenly came to herself, amazing the doctors. Her mind was clear and she was perfectly fine. The Lord had restored her to her husband and children."[87]

This happened because God "called" this pastor's wife to a place of crisis intercession and she obediently persevered until breakthrough happened. Her *rest* was not more important to her than the *rescue*. She knew God would sustain her while she was on the "night shift", shifting the atmosphere from mourning to morning for that woman and her family.

Can You Wear This Armor?

When David was preparing to go out and fight the giant Goliath, he needed a suit of armor. King Saul offered his own armor for David to wear. Of course, it did not fit him. He was not ready to be king yet, but what he was ready for, was to wear and inner armor that suited him to stand against any foe and believe that he and God (not in that order of course), were unbeatable. It's not what you wear as a title on the outside of your clothes. What *does* matter is the heart you have that is *possessed* by God, to overcome the darkness of our day and those days to come. You *need* an indomitable faith. Stay in the word of God. Keep reading stories that build you up. Don't be discouraged by adverse winds. They come, but fight them with the faith you build daily and expect change to happen. "Be not

---

[87] Dutch Sheets, Dutch Sheets, *The Beginner's Guide to Intercessory Prayer* (Ventura Calif: Regal, 2008),119

weary in well doing", you shall reap, if you faint not!" (Galatians 6:7 KJV)

Final Thoughts

Are You A Crisis Intercessor?

1. Are you commonly awakened with an urgent need to pray about a person, place or problem?

2. In your regular times of prayer, are you often struck with the sense of a pending emergency?

3. Do you thrive in times of crisis?

4. Is your daily routine often interrupted with a call to pray about a face, a name or a situation you have witnessed?

5. Do you find you have no rest in prayer until the crisis is over or until you have the assurance that your assignment is completed? [88]

---

[88] Alves, Intercessors, 142

Chapter 14 The Governmental Intercessor

You and I have heard it time and time again, "Religion and Politics don't mix." Our expectations then become, that we should let the world run the political realm, and as believers we should be quiet and just go to church. However, this is such an anti-biblical mentality. Let's begin by sharing a few scriptures and then we will move on to provoking you in your prayer life. Make no mistake about it, all of us are called to pray for those who govern our cities and nation. Some however, have a passion for it that leads them to doing it daily and often. It stays on their heart. Are you one of those persons? Let's validate you with the Word. Rest assured, you are not an illegitimate intercessor and you should not be in hiding. Although this is not the extent of governmental intercession, it is an important piece.

And Now, A Word From our Sponsor

Psalm 22:28 KJV says, "For the kingdom is the Lord's: and he is the governor among all nations."

Daniel 4:17 KJV "This matter is by the decree of the watchers, and the demand by the word of the holy ones: to the intent that the living may know that the most High ruleth in the kingdom of men, and giveth it to whomsoever he will, and setteth up over it the basest of men."

Romans 13:1-4 KJV "Let every soul be subject unto the higher powers. For there is no power but of God: the powers that be are ordained of God.[2] Whosoever therefore resisteth the power, resisteth the ordinance of God: and they that resist shall receive to themselves damnation.[3] For rulers are not a terror to good works, but to the evil. Wilt thou then not be afraid of the power? do that which is good, and thou shalt have praise of the same:[4] For he is the minister of God to thee for good. But if thou do that which is evil, be afraid; for he beareth not the sword in vain: for he is the minister of God, a revenger to execute wrath upon him that doeth evil."

I Timothy 2:1-4 "I exhort therefore, that, first of all, supplications, prayers, intercessions, and giving of thanks, be made for all men;[2] For kings, and for all that are in authority; that we may lead a quiet and peaceable life in all godliness and honesty.[3] For this is good and acceptable in the sight of God our Saviour;[4] Who will have all men to be saved, and to come unto the knowledge of the truth."

When we read these scriptures we become aware that God rules over the destinies of rulers and their nations. And yet, he exercises his rule through his people. What God makes happen in the earth, he makes it happen through us. How? It's simple, we effect everything, beginning in the unseen world. We pray, speaking things into existence, and we work to place ourselves in positions of influence as well.

Church and State

English Political philosopher John Locke is often credited with the concept of separating church and state, however even before him, Protestant Reformer Martin Luther began writing about the "Doctrine of two Kingdoms." He taught (as the bible also teaches) that God was the ruler of the whole world and that he rules in two ways: secular *and* heavenly government. When Locke wrote his treatise on "The Social Contract," he wanted to speak to the dangers of the government having too much authority over the people. His position was that it should not dictate the spiritual or religious beliefs of the people. Formal President Thomas Jefferson, referencing the first Amendment wrote that he believed that religion was a matter which lies between man and his God, and that he did not owe an account to anyone else regarding his faith or practice of worship. He admonished that there be a "wall of separation" between church and state, so the government would not interfere with religion.

This is all very interesting and good. Notice, the state should not influence the church and yet we see in our daily affairs, that it does. Decisions of the state effect everything! Daily we are seeing more and more moral issues come before our legislators. They generally rule on the side of two things: the feelings of the voter base; and secondly, their personal or family convictions/ orientation/ influences. The former often wins out, especially when the ambitious who desire to keep their job, please their party, or get promotions, are considering their future.

Bi-Partisan Intercession

The governmental intercessor cannot be in political bondage. They cannot be an idol worshipper. If you are so tied to a "donkey" or an "elephant," that you cannot be guided by the "Lamb," your intercession will be of no or little effect.

Your heart will not be able to allow you to effectively, sincerely attack clearly designated evil, standing to protect truth. There is good and evil on both sides of the aisle in politics. And even though the state should not dictate what we do in religious affairs, we should effect everything *they* do with our intercession. Isaiah 9:6 KJV says, "For unto us a child is born, unto us a son is given: and the government shall be upon his shoulder: and his name shall be called Wonderful, Counsellor, The mighty God, The everlasting Father, The Prince of Peace". Isaiah prophesies of Christ. He came and deposited Himself in a corporate body of believers called, "Ecclesia", the called out ones; body of Christ; the anointed ones with *His* anointing. The government is upon His shoulder, through us. We carry the responsibility to establish His Kingdom in the earth. That means, effect any and every alternative government. **His** government is our cross to **share**, the world's government is our cross to "**bear**." Both the carrying and the sharing are heavy burdens that require intimacy with the Father in order to fulfill.

Too often, we elect government officials and do not hold them accountable to the standards we believe or they say they have. Too often our excuse is, "Well, they are not pastors, are they?" The obvious answer is, no, but are they not Christians? If they are indeed Christians, shouldn't they believe they were placed in certain environments to help establish the Kingdom of God on earth?

"The Bible says that a government official is God's servant for your good (Romans 13:4 ESV), but how can government officials effectively serve God if no one is allowed to tell them what they believe God expects of them? The Bible says that government officials are sent "to punish those who do evil and to praise them who do good" (1st Peter 2:14 ESV), but how can they do that if no spokesman from the world's religions are allowed to give then counsel on what is good and what is "evil?"[89]

The Heart of the Intercessor

Every intercessor's heart must be just like Jesus. The writer of Hebrews says that..." He always lives to make intercession"... for those who need to, and actually do draw near to God the Father. Prayer for people, is the very breath of an intercessor. To cease praying is to cut off our oxygen. To watch tragedy or trouble and be like a bystander is not optional. What is the purpose of a true fan at a game, if when the team is down you never give them a boost? The difference however, between a sports fan and an intercessor for the kingdom of God, is that we never leave the game early, giving up any hope of our team winning.

No one had to tell Aaron and Hur to intercede for their leader in the time of battle. They knew, if his hands went down because of exhaustion, their nation would be defeated. They were not on the front line of the physical battlefield, but their assignment was no less important. The frontline troops got their inspiration from the strength of their leader. The leader's sustained strength was in the hands of the intercessors.

David Bradshaw, the leader of "The Prayer Furnace," in Fredericksburg, VA shared a dream he had at the recent (2013) Awaken the Dawn Conference. He said that in the dream, he was having lunch at the White House with President Obama. After they finished having lunch and talking about various issues, they got in the car and he started driving President Obama around. Not long after he had that dream, he spoke to a friend who is also a part of another 24 hour House of Prayer. Someone from their House of Prayer had the same exact dream. As they began to unpack the meaning of the dream (discussing it), God revealed to them that they were driving the

---

[89] Wayne Grudem, *Politics According to the Bible: a Comprehensive Resource for Understanding Modern Political Issues in Light of Scripture* (Grand Rapids, Mich.: Zondervan, 2010), 35

purpose/will of God in the President's heart by prayer. They in essence, as they pray for the president became Aaron and Hur types. While they may not get Joshua notoriety, none the less, victory does not come without their being on post. Is this not one of the assignments of EVERY child of God, let alone the government intercessor? It is often the heart and effort of the unseen and unsung heroes that have made the difference in the lives of all of us. Make no mistake about it, you, my dear friend, bring a valuable asset to the table.

Government: God's Priority

Let's look at I Timothy 2:1-4 KJV, which says, " I exhort therefore, that, first of all, supplications, prayers, intercessions, and giving of thanks, be made for all men; For kings, and for all that are in authority; that we may lead a quiet and peaceable life in all godliness and honesty. For this is good and acceptable in the sight of God our Saviour; Who will have all men to be saved, and to come unto the knowledge of the truth".

Derek Prince is right when he says, "After all men," the first specific topic for prayer is "Kings, and…all that are in authority." In countries such as the United States, which have no monarchy, the word "Kings" does not apply on any case, whether there be a monarchy or not, the phrase "all that are in authority" indicates all those who are responsible for governing the nation. This may be summed up in the single word: "the government." [90]

Prince goes on to state what most Christians are guilty of and probably need to repent of. It is undoubtedly the sin of omission. We pray regularly for many things, but the first thing we are admonished to pray for here in 1st Timothy 2, is

---

[90] Derek Prince, *Shaping History through Prayer and Fasting* (New Kensington, PA: Whitaker House, 2002),48

government. He says, "When praying for government, what specific petition are we exhorted to make? In the second verse, Paul answered, That one may live a quiet and peaceable life in all godliness and honesty! Does the government we live under affect the way we live? Obviously it does. Therefore, if we desire a good way of life, logic and self-interest alike indicate that we should pray for our government."[91]

God's Purpose for Prayer

Of course, if you are at this level, you already know that prayer has a purpose. And yet, many people have no clue what it is. Prayer is a means to an end. There are examples from cover to cover in scripture, of examples of prayer and the results of it. However, often when we are praying, so many people merely go through the motions without the fully expected end in mind. I am not just talking about unanswered prayer, but rather ***being*** prayer and ***the*** answer. Let me explain it this way by offering you my description of the purpose of prayer.

Several years ago I was privileged to write a book (that I recommend you purchase and read) entitled, *"I Am The Church, And My Name is House of Prayer."* In it, I spelled out the four-fold purpose of prayer.

1. To Learn the Language of Heaven- Heaven has a language! Initially when we learn to pray, we should not learn to pray, merely imitating the language of men. We should simply be using the WORD OF GOD. We should use the models that Jesus and other prayer warrior gave. However, when the baptism of Holy Spirit came, their entered another realm of heavens prayers. We moved from the flesh realm to the Spirit realm. "It sounds strange to be speaking of a higher

---

[91]Ibid, 49

language than the Word of God. What could be purer? Well, in reality...nothing. However, because God looks at words as meaningless without spirit, would it not be possible, even probable, to speak Gods' Word without the interruption or corruption of human flesh? What if you could pray His heart, Word, Will, without human flesh interventions or demonic interception?" [92] Well, there is a language heaven understands and it cannot be interrupted by us or Satan. It's the language of Holy Spirit. When He dwells within, He comes with a language you have a right to use, that is special and pure. It is therefore Word based and Kingdom driven

2. To Communicate with Our Father- While God was here in the earth, in the person of Jesus, He taught us how to properly communicate with Him. Is that awesome or what? He took matters in His own hands and said, "This is how I want you to communicate with me so that you can have the results of a Kingdom ambassador. You are designed to have authority". That is why the disciples, in Luke 11:1 asked Jesus, "Lord Teach Us To Pray." They knew that the key to everything they needed was in their ability to communicate with the Father."[93]

3. To Be Turned Into the Image of His Dear Son (and my brother) - That image is suppose to look like Genesis 1:27-28, which says

> "So God created man in his own image, in the image of God created he him; male and female

---

[92] Darryl Husband, *I Am the Church and My Name Is House of Prayer* (Richmond, VA: lulu.com, 2011), 29

[93] Ibid.,36

created he them. 28 And God blessed them, and God said unto them, Be fruitful, and multiply, and replenish the earth, and subdue it: and have dominion over the fish of the sea, and over the fowl of the air, and over every living thing that moveth upon the earth".

Jesus *lived* the splitting image of and perfect description of that Genesis passage. Unlike Adam, he never wavered. Hebrews 1:3, in the NIV says, "The Son is the radiance of God's glory and the exact representation of his being, sustaining all things by his powerful word. After he had provided purification for sins, he sat down at the right hand of the Majesty in heaven."

4. And Effect a Transformation In The Earth Realm

Wayne Grudem says, "It seems to me the, "do evangelism, not politics," view, has a mistaken understanding of what is important to God, as if only spiritual (non-material, other worldly) things matter to Him and not the actual circumstances of people's physical life in this world."[94] My response to that is an obvious AMEN! If God didn't care what happens in the world, why send prophets to Kings? Did he not create us? Did he not desire to see King Saul successful as ruler of His people, then desired him to be replaced. His job was to effect a change in the lives of the people so their heart would either stay with or be returned, to God

The Seed of Un-Surrendered Government

---

[94] Grudem, *Politics According to the Bible: a Comprehensive Resource for Understanding Modern Political Issues in Light of Scripture*.47

I still love black and white movies. It was there where I first saw "cops and robbers" stories. Whenever anyone was caught by the police or a sheriff in the old west, the law officers would say those famous words, "get your hands up." Sometimes, when a person knew they were outnumbered, beaten, or just not strong enough to go against their opponent in a battle, they would raise their hands high and surrender. It was to say to their captor or opponent, "I am under your authority. Take me where ever you wish."

Politics is often the real civil war. Parties spend their time trying to figure out ways to frustrate the other and live by an unwritten code in our day: "I will never surrender." I believe that a nation that has no moral standards is writing its own death warrant. The philosopher Epictetus once said, "God has given us a name, and we have sought to change it."

Paul writes in the Book of Romans, "We have gone about to establish our own righteousness and not the righteousness of God. (Romans 10:3, KJV). When this takes place, it is a sign of several things. One of those things is this: God is looking for people who will save His people from their waywardness, but he can't find them. How can it be said, "The harvest is plentiful, but the laborers are few?" (Matthew 9:38 KJV) Is that true as well in our generation? You *have* to answer that.

Governmental Intercessors are warfare/prophetic intercessors that have been assigned to a strategic location. They are Special Forces. You must get the enemy to surrender. Ephesians 6:12 KJV says, "For we wrestle not against flesh and blood, but against principalities, against powers, against the rulers of the darkness of this world, against spiritual wickedness in high places." Therefore, our fight is not with people. We do not have to be around them to win. We effect the powers of the air by our intercession. If we are not constantly bombarding them with aerial attacks, their seed will fall unhindered in the earth. The harvest of seed that is "unsurrendered" to the will of God, has already been seen. Just read Genesis, chapter 3. Let me give you two other accounts, one from the Old, one from the New Testament, of government that sowed "unsurrendered" seed and the harvest that ensued. After we see those, let's view today's government.

Pharaoh

In the book of Exodus, we meet a Ruler/King/Pharaoh who was "unsurrendered" to the will of God. His government was unacceptable to God. God chose to send Moses to bring deliverance to the people in bondage. Proverbs 29:2 says, "When the wicked rule, the people mourn." However, strangely enough, the people in bondage had been there so long, that they did not even know they were in mourning. All mourning is not in ones visible emotions. Your attitude may be in a state of mourning by merely accepting a place where you are, when you were born to be in another. Your spirit man is in mourning, but your flesh is so accustomed to bondage it has become master to it (the spirit mom). Therefore your spirit man grieves in utter silence, hoping for a rescue, but knowing there will be a battle to convince the flesh (mind, intellect, emotions, will), that freedom is better, and ONLY God, has that answer.

Pharaoh had the children of God dependent upon *his* government for all of their needs. When you hear them speak, even after deliverance, they sound like they are still in bondage. They were "*free*" slaves, not slaves that had been set free. They knew they were not born for bondage, but whenever trouble confronted them, they reverted to the option of returning to Egypt. They *never* fully "surrendered" to God. The government of Pharaoh had planted such a powerful seed of "Neediness" in them, that they never left the "demand" side of life, to be on the "supply" side. They died with a rebellious, complaining, contentious, fearful, poverty mentality. Pharaoh's seed destroyed a generation of Gods' children. They could not or would not kill that seed.

And yet, God sent a governmental intercessor to help them with their issues. Moses spent his life interceding for Israel. At one glance, he was unsuccessful. At a second glance, it appears that he was not. He died before he reached his designation. He lost a generation in the wilderness on the way to his destination. But he also raised up a Joshua and another generation, that would eventually make it without the dragging of the chains of their past. All success is not apparent. Do not try to make the judgment alone. Let God determine that. You stay focused on your assignment.

Herod

In the book of Matthew, Government Leader Herod, has heard about Jesus and His birth into the world. He believes the report. Now I think that is pretty phenomenal. A King that is paranoid about a child born into his region that may threaten his kingdom, decided to have all the children killed (at a certain age and under). Can you imagine the terror in that region? The tension of parents? The anger? The depression?

Dutch Sheets writes, "One of the New Testament words for destiny is *"horizo."* In this Greek word, it is easy to see the English word "horizon", which is the point where the earth and the sky meet. *Horizo* also means a boundary, because the concept of a horizon involves the farthest limits of sight. It doesn't take much imagination to see the concept of destiny in the Word. Our destiny is our God-given horizon or boundary. God has predetermined the *boundaries* or *horizons* of our lives. He has predestined the plans and purpose He has for each of us, before we were even born."[95]

"Unsurrendered" governments do not value the seed nor its potential, unless it has immediate or **very** prosperous future benefits. If it threatens the status quo or has potential to over

---

[95] Sheets, Beginners Guide to Intercessory Prayer, 49

throw (good or bad) the present governmental thinking, then Abort!

The Issues of Our Day

I was sitting around a lunch table recently with a group of pastors who are from different denominational backgrounds and political affiliations. One of them raised the question why there was so much concern about this issue of homosexuality and same sex marriages and not other issues. My response was (also echoed by a few others), that gay marriage, abortion and poverty are the hot topics of our day. Just as war on drugs, women's right to vote, racial discrimination and others were in the forefront at other times. It is not that any of those things have gone totally away, but there are times some issues are more *toxic* than others and need addressing before they destroy or at least distract our purpose, and destiny as a people.

1. Abortion- Lack of understanding when life begins and our commitment to God to protect the life of the unborn

2. Gay Marriage- The complete defiance of Gods plan to multiply us in the earth

3. Poverty- The lack of resources, jobs, skills, Initiative to sustain a moderate life

4. Race- Color division, cultural ignorance that causes us to see one another as enemies rather than family. The inability to recognize that all have the same Father (God) and originates from the same home (genetics conclude that a village in West Africa is the cradle of civilization)

Whenever any party is in the White House, government intercessors must be careful not to become blinded by: first of their kind (African American, Latino, Women, Native American); the famous (Charismatic Leaders who become the popular stars of our day); the fortunate (well off people in the time of recession); or anyone else. Governmental intercessors are stuck on **God** and **truth**, Period!

When *Right*, Rules

No one party has it *ALL* right. I know they all think they do, but we all know better. You hear voters often say, "I am just going to vote for the lesser of two evils." Governmental Intercessors are the evil eradicators. They pray to God for what's called, a "breakers anointing." It is the praying in the realm of the apostolic. This means, to pray for order, truth, rights or righteousness to be established in the seat of government (both parties)   Colossians 1:27 (NIV) says, " ...Christ in you the hope of Glory." That said, you *are* the burden bearing, yoke breaking power of God sent to the earth, in time to effect the destiny of governments. The question is, Do **you** Know that?

Governmental intercessors are called to pray righteous people into positions as well. "When the righteous are in authority, the people rejoice..." (Proverbs 29:2). Every governmental intercessor should be praying for God to raise up Kings like Asa (save his one error), who was the first king mentioned, that did what was good in the eyes of The Lord. He had a 10 year run that was spectacular.

II Kings 23:7 says, "And he brake down the houses of the Sodomites, that were by the house of the Lord, where the women wove hangings for the grove."

And Deuteronomy23:17 says, "There shall be no whore of the daughters of Israel, nor a sodomite of the sons of Israel."

The Call to Serve *Our* King

Everyone is called to serve. We serve in various ways. We do it by offering ourselves to others in ways that will meet *their* needs and bring pleasure to *them* in the long run. By helping them, we are in essence helping others, because it improves the capacity of the one we are serving, to be able to improve their life, health, finances and emotions. All of this helps them to help others in a greater way.

Governmental intercessors serve others from their knees, their face, (prostrate), or standing with outstretched arms. Whatever the posture may be, what is essentially important, is what we *say*. Here is where and how and why you serve:

1. Your Community- We are called to pray for the place we live. It's our Jerusalem. We must pray for its peace. Our local city council and school reps as well as our city leaders must be interceded for constantly. They effect our way of life Our school board representatives determines the educational development of our children, and whether they will have the tools to help them compete in the next generation. Our children and their abilities determine community growth and safety. Do you know the names of your city council person, county supervisor, and school board representatives?

2. Your City- Is your mayor or chairperson of the board of supervisors on your list? What about the other leaders in your city, county, town? Do you have a list of the most politically influential people in your area? They all may not be politicians. They may be attorneys, judges, business people, philanthropists, a local retiree, president of residence council, civic chair in a neighborhood, even a pastor. They should all be on your prayer list. Jeremiah 29:7 says, "And seek the peace of the city whither I have caused you to be

carried away captives, and pray unto the Lord for it: for in the peace thereof shall ye have peace."

3. Your State Leaders- Governors, Senators, and Delegates or Representatives.

4. Our President and Cabinets as well as Armed Forces leaders, World leaders Proverbs 11:14 says, "Where no counsel is, the people fall: but in the multitude of counselors there is safety.

Prayer Focus

1. For Heart change or to be lined up with the Word-That Nobody but Jesus sits on the throne room of their heart.

2. For constituents to know the issues and the will of God (according to His Word) and vote the bible.

3. For constituents to hold politicians accountable.

4. For political representatives to be free from party pressure.

5. For the exit of unrighteous people, who will not be transformed in their thinking.

Add your list here...
6.

7.

8.

Did you fill in any blanks? What could you pray for?

Daniel 2:20-22 KJV "Daniel answered and said, Blessed be the name of God for ever: for wisdom and might are his: 21 And he changeth the times and the seasons: he removeth kings, and setteth up kings: he giveth wisdom unto the wise, and knowledge to them that know understanding: 22 He revealeth the deep and secret things: he knoweth what is in the darkness, and the light dwelleth with him.

Thy Kingdom Come

The purpose of government intercessors is to stand on God's side as watchmen over politicians *and* church leaders that represent the various countries, states, cities, neighborhoods, homes, schools and churches in the earth. Make no mistake about what we are here for: to establish HIS KINGDOM in the earth. That cannot happen if the church is not the standard bearer, leading by way of intercession. The Greek philosopher Aristotle wrote, "The state comes into existence that man may live. It continues that men may live well: But man can only live well when God is in control."

If this is so, as we intimated already, then governmental intercessors must be partners with the "Bridal" intercessors, praying for the church to stay in order. When the church is out of order, so too will be, the world. *We* are the glory carriers. *We* are the match that ignites the torch of *"Thy Kingdom Come, Thy Will Be Done..."* Matthew 6:10 KJV

According to Genesis 9:25, Canaan was once a cursed land, but we now know it as the promised land. It *became* that. Jerusalem as well, was once a stronghold for giants, but the city *called* Jeru-salem *became* its name, "city of peace". God can do it Again! Do you believe that?

He is asking *you* my friend, these ancient but relevant questions, Can these bones live? Is there no balm in Gilead? He is asking if there is someone who will stand in the gaps for your city, town, county, state, and nation. I declare, That the statement in Ezekiel 22:30 (KJV), will not be said of us, ***"...but He could not find ONE."*** What do you say? Come on Intercessors, Declare, "Not On My Watch!"

Are You A Government Intercessor?

Well get on your post and stay there! Here are a few questions you may need to consider as you go forward:

1. How often do you watch the news?

2. Do you keep up with the passing of bills?

3. Do you read your local new paper?

4. Do you check on the legislative issues of your city?

5. Do you know the names of the key spiritual leaders in your city?

6. What denominations are strong there?

7. What are the key spiritual issues in your area?

Chapter 15 The General Intercessor: The Decathlete of Intercession

When I was growing up, all the doctors I knew of in our community were what we called, "general practitioners." You went to those doctors for every kind of problem no matter what it was or you dealt with it at home. As a matter of fact, you may even cal many of our mothers and grandmothers "unlicensed" general practitioners. They often diagnosed cases of ailment in the home, often because they did not have the financial resources to go to the doctor. The general practitioners (licensed and unlicensed) were the ones that prescribed what you needed to get well. no one cared like they cared. It seemed as though they had all the answers. Everything that you needed to deal with what may have been wrong with you, the general practitioner could handle it. I am certain that they had specialists working in the hospital, but they were not the popular people group they are today. Specialist were there as guests in the room, but the general practitioner, who was also known as the family physician, *was,* like family. I still remember my doctor and where my doctor's office was when I was a child. I was in the hospital for double pneumonia as a child and for tonsillitis as an adult. I do not remember the names of my anesthesiologist, or the surgeon. I do not even remember any specialists coming to see me when I had pneumonia. I do however remember my "primary care physician." Dr. Jackson when I was young and Dr. Cummings as an adult, were really as I mentioned, like family.

Intercessory Schizophrenia

As we begin this chapter I want you to expect that you will see the area of the general intercessor much like the general practitioner. You may have been reading this book, coming to each area of intercession saying one of two things to yourself: (1) "That's not me. Ok, that's not my area of passion either." or, (2) "Yes, that's me right there. I am a worship intercessor," then getting to the prophetic intercession saying the same thing, "Oh yes, I'm a prophetic intercessor." Then the governmental intercessor looks like you because you have a passion to pray for the president and maybe local officials at times. So you are now trying to figure out whether you are an "intercessory schizophrenic." I mean, which one of those DNAs are in you is a mystery, or are they all? Well, if you've been troubled by this, have no fear. Settle down. You are not crazy. You are unique, special and very valuable. If you've been troubled by finding out which one of those you are categorized as, but many of them are in your DNA it is probably because you are a general intercessor. Again, have no fear. Park your car right here. This means that you are the helper of every area of intercession and are a valuable commodity.

In baseball you are the pinch-hitter in the ninth inning. When the game is on the line, the coach can depend upon you to come in the game and take care of business. You are the first person off the bench in the basketball game when somebody is needed to defend, or score an offensive barrage. You are the person that is called upon at any given time as the most gifted. You are a multi-dimensional player. Some would call you a role player. You can be depended upon to cover many areas. Your value cannot be put in words. Teams do not win championships without you. You are an all-around athlete that can play any position. That is what the general intercessor is likened unto. You are God's utility player. The team Must have you to win.

So my beloved, let's get started and uncover this very important area called, "General Intercession."

I Have No Agenda, But God's

The general intercessor really has no agenda. When we say that, we do not mean to suggest that there is no order or clue in what they are going to pray from day to day or moment to moment in their prayer time. On the contrary my beloved, their plate is usually the most full of all intercessors. They never go to prayer with an agenda of their own however, except that the agenda be given to them by God. And God often calls on us to carry others into prayer. It is very important that the General intercessor understand that God is the giver of agendas. As you begin your prayer time, your prayer time will possibly be spent with a list of names of people and people groups, cities, countries or special regions of the world. There are a variety of things on the general intercessors list. Again, the agenda is, "I don't have an agenda." This is really leaving the door open for God to give you anything at anytime, to intercede about. As a matter of fact, it's really the agenda of others that often becomes today's agenda. Today's agenda may be to back up the crisis intercessors. It may be that today you are praying the heart of what is going on in the area of financial intercession.

What's the Diagnosis?

The general intercessor must know the elements of its community its church and its society as a whole. Therefore, contact with the research intercessors is critical. You are born into the Intercessory family to necessarily to diagnose every ailment, but to help the diagnosis come forth and then pray for the prescription that brings healing. General intercessors are the workhorse of intercession. The jack of all trades. You are the Mr. And Mrs. Fix it. "I can handle!" "Nothing is too hard for me." So I repeat, to diagnose those ailments and then prescribe through prayer those things that will bring healing is what you are made of. If you get pressured when things get tight, this may not be your area.

I Have Your Back

We have called this area "general" intercessors. Maybe we should call it the "Generals" of intercession as well. The general intercessor has no problem leading. They do not have a specific area of passion, so they do not have to wait for their number to be called. They lead and cover every other area. They are encouragers, troop rally leaders. Therefore, this area of general intercession may be the most important area of all the intercessors for one reason, they cover everybody else's back. Because they do not have what we call a specific area of intercession, they actually *carry* the other intercessors. So, today, I want to take time to honor our general intercessors. We live in a day and age where everybody puts its emphasis on and cheers on those persons who are specialist. However, we need to still have room for the general practitioner and general intercessor.

Whosoever and Whatsoever Will, Come On
The Decathlete of Intercession

General Intercessors pray for everybody, at anytime, about anything.

They may liken their team to be called the "Baskin Robbins" team. We don't specialize in any one flavor, but you can count on us to have them all and be satisfied with your visit. Maybe it's even more like Burger King's little jingle, "...special orders don't upset us. All we ask is that you let us have it *your* way.

The general intercessor, although they are a group in itself, they really should be categorized as we said earlier as a utility person. However, that may not give some of you a healthy perspective if you played or studied baseball, so let me go one better. Let me liken the general intercessor to the Olympic decathlete who is called the world's greatest athlete. They have to be the most well conditioned and well rounded of all athletes. Their training is extensive. They do not have to be great at any one sport or event. As a matter of fact, they probably wouldn't qualify for an open individual event. They are not necessarily good enough to be world class runners or discus throwers, but not one of those persons in individual events could do what they do in 10 events.

The general intercessors may even be called the "*intercessors*" intercessor. They are the burden bearers of intercession; the intercessory cross carriers. They often say to other intercessory prayer groups, "I have you!" "I got this for you!" Jesus was just like that, was He not? He never cared about what a person's condition was, the background the person came from or the age of the person. Whatever condition he came across He just said, "Whosoever will, let them come." "Let the children come unto me." "The well have not a need of a physician." When the Pharisees came to him saying, "Why do you heal on the Sabbath day? He mentioned to them that the Sabbath was made for man not man for the Sabbath.

There was no condition too great for Jesus to handle. He was never burdened by, nor did he hide from a condition. Such is the life and posture of the general intercessor. Just like Jesus could be called an apostle, prophet, evangelist, pastor, teacher, having all of the fivefold ministry gifts, so does the general intercessor.

"The Request Lines Are Now Open "

When I was a young boy I used to sit up late at night with my uncle Michael listening to the radio. Of course, don't tell my father, we were both supposed to be asleep because we had school the next day. He is five years my senior so as a high school student he had girls and love songs on his mind. I probably picked up too much of both from him during those years (however the love songs did help me shape my worship mentality as I shifted to the Kingdom of God many years later). Often at night, before the radio stations in the city of Chicago and Gary Indiana (which we could pick up), would go off the air, who would tell all of the listeners of their station that the lines would now be open for requests. People would then call in and asking for their favorite song to be played and lo and behold, he would find those songs and meet the emotional need of the persons who were calling. The audiences all around the city had their favorite disc jockeys. They got to know many callers by their voices and called their names out over the airways, dedicating songs to them.

Much like those disc jockeys are the general intercessors. They too take prayer requests. The one difference is, that the radio stations closed for the night and after a song was played, that was it. They didn't get intimately involved in the life of the caller outside of their name and their voice. The general intercessor carries the caller's name , voice and burden and dedicates the prayer to them and those they desire prayer for. They do not leave the callers request until it is answered. For instance, the disc jockey would give a "shout out" to the person the song was dedicated to, helping a love connection for *that* moment alone. Then they move on to the next caller and that last call is forgotten unless they are a regular. They don't get involved in the *real* life experiences of the callers. Why would they? It's just a job, right?

Well, not so, with the general intercessor. It is not just a job. It is an assignment on one's life. Intimacy is what you do. Once you begin praying for an area, you can't release it until you are satisfied that it has been settled in the heavenlies.

Ok, go ahead and declare in the atmosphere, "The lines are now open. Call me with whatever request you have and we will pray that prayer through to the end." The general intercessor keeps a list of things for which they pray. They take prayer requests with pleasure.

"Let's Head It Off At the Path"

The old cowboy movies used to fascinate me as a child. I remember the *Lone Ranger* being one of my favorites. Every so often he and Tonto would be chasing some bad guy and would see them heading a certain way. Sitting atop a ridge, they would look down and say, "Let's head them off at the path." They saw which way the adversary was going and moved ahead to catch them off guard.

The general intercessor must practice the art of preventive care, much like the general practitioner, one of the assignments of the general intercessor is to keep the world from getting sick, not just reacting *to* sickness. Elisha was so in tune with God and humanity, that he could hear where the enemy was headed. he was like the Lone Ranger and Tonto. "Let's head them off at the path." The King, of Aram was so troubled by the preparation for his attacks and his defeats by the people of God, that he through his own men that he thought his own men were spying on him. When he questioned their, loyalty they responded with the utmost respect for the man of God. 2Kings 6:12(NIV) says, "None of us, my lord the king," said one of his officers, "but Elisha, the prophet who is in Israel, tells the king of Israel the very words you speak in your bedroom."

The general intercessor sees a problem and covers the problem before it becomes a critical concern. Therefore they operate as well, as a prophetic intercessor in that they begin to pray things into existence rather than waiting for crisis to *happen.* Here is where the crisis intercessor needs to, and should partner with, the prophetic and general intercessor.

They need seers so that they can *prevent* crisis and not just react *to* crisis. The general as well as the prophetic (seer) intercessor, begins to pray about a particular issue, seeing that it *may* take place. They see the problem and possibility. The problem for them then is that it becomes as a seed that will produce a particular harvest. They must diagnose the problem, provide the antidote of prayer and sound the alarm to the other troops. They send the prayer through like the general practitioner, believing that if the patient begins to deal with this issue now, the problem will not grow. It will subside.

However, if for some reason the preventive care falls through, and that issue becomes a crisis or problem, like the general practitioner, the general intercessor never panics. They get in there as a team player with the crisis intercessor and take care of the problem.

" This Is A Job For Superman"

I remember one of my favorite shows and characters growing up, was Superman of course I loved to watch Batman as well. I remember being glued to the television seeing the trouble the people were facing and waiting for that one line to be said by someone: "This is a job for, Superman." Or hear Commissioner Gordon say, "Where is Batman." The general intercessor may not see themselves as a superhero, but a partner with the superhero. Like Commissioner Gordon may flash lights in the sky for Batman to show up, the general intercessor knows that there are times while he or she is praying that they need to solicit the help of a specialist. We all need help, even the so called, "*helpers*." Therefore the general intercessors are also a referral Intercessory team. Of course by that we do not mean that they pass all areas of intercession or prayer requests off to others they think are better qualified. It means that they are always partnering with a particular Intercessory Group to pray with them. They believe in **team** (**T**ogether **E**very **A**im **M**et). So you to need to know and understand when to hand off a specific area to a specialized group or person on your team. The Bible says, "Again I say unto you, That if two of you shall agree on earth as touching anything that they shall ask, it shall be done for them of my Father which is in heaven." (Matt 18:19 KJV)   One can put a thousand to flight and two ten thousand. Together the word in Genesis is said of us, but in a positive manner, "now nothing they have imagined will be impossible!" (Gen. 11: 5-6)

A Degree in General Studies

When I was in college, there were a many students who came to school and began their college career not knowing what they wanted to study. They didn't declare a major sometimes for years. they took a bunch of classes and may have been the most well rounded students in the school. They were categorized each year by the hours they took just as I was. Their major was general studies which meant they had the opportunity to study everything. If they declared a major it was usually because they *knew* they enjoyed an area of discipline and would focus in on it, not just guessing like most of us were.

I want to suggest to you as a general intercessor that you study every area of intercession so that nothing ever surprises you. When you do that you can go deeper than most intercessors and stretch wider in your prayers. General Intercessory prayer warriors should always be looking for the sociological, psychological and even biological issues that are involved in the areas of a person or people group. You should be interested in what is the core issue here. Why are you dealing with these issues (again going back to the partnership with the research intercessor).

I mentioned in an earlier chapter that many persons come to the doctor and they are looking for a diagnosis for something that they're dealing with and the doctor immediately puts them on some medication take for the rest of their lives. The general intercessor is not interested in just diving in to pray without knowing root causes. They want deliverance not just a bandage to hide the wound. He or she looks at every people group searching for ways to break their chains of bondage. As the song writer says, "There is power in the name of Jesus... to break every chain. There is an army rising up, to break every chain... I hear the chains falling..."

Revival Now

The general intercessor is always looking for revival. They have excellence in their heart. Their desire is to see order, healing, oneness, deliverance, love, dominion and great faith resorted in the body so that it can function as Kingdom ambassadors in the world. They pray for revival constantly inside the body so that the body can bring revival to the world.

"Musts" of The General Intercessor

As we close this chapter, it is very important to that we drive home a few final nails that we may have hammered but not tapped out. The general intercessor must:

1. Be persevering: has to pray every issue through until God says stop. Perseverance is not common enough in this generation. People are moving around constantly from job to job, church to church, relationship to relationship, searching for magic formulas instead of working diligently at making where they are work. There is nothing like seeing the end result of hard work.

2. Love all people from all backgrounds. You are a servant of all. It is very difficult or almost impossible to really pray or serve anyone if you do not love them. If there is a lack of love in any area for any people God is calling for you to pray for, the enemy will cause your prayers to be ineffective. You will stand for the blood

of those people. they are your responsibility. do not take that lightly. You should begin to pray for them now as a matter of fact. Here is what I've discovered. You cannot truly pray for anybody over a period of time and not change your heart about them. Even if you have a disdain for their character or politics, you will love ***them*** as a person enough to pray them into their divine destiny.

3. Work under pressure. Anytime you have the weight of the other teams of soldiers in your back you ***know*** that is pressure. it's like the team captain. *Everyone* depends on you. so my dear friend, understand that your assignment in the area intercession calls for you to have to "endure hard times like a good soldier."

4. Be a team player; I mentioned earlier, in so many words, that the general intercessor has to be a sociable person. They have to be in communication with and call on other areas of intercession to help them as well as always ready to be called on by those groups to get their job done.

5. Know that discipline is critical. All people need disciplined lives. The general intercessor is no different. However, it is virtually impossible for the general intercessor to be effective if they do not exercise a great deal of discipline. He/she must have time management down pat. They must have a schedule and keep it. Often, the general intercessor because of the content of their area, ends up being very lengthy in their time of prayer. They cannot pray for one hour and then just stop. Their intercession does not end. They are ALWAYS carrying someone else's cross.

6. Have an inquiring mind. The general intercessor is always asking questions. How can I serve you? What is

on your prayer agenda? What is the condition? Has it manifested yet? What is the vision? What are your expectations? They are people as we mentioned earlier who face every situation with expectation and pray the future over people

7. Be all things to all people, as we mentioned earlier, they are a little bit of everything. They live by the words the Apostle Paul writes in First Corinthians 9:19-23 (NIV),

> [19] Though I am free and belong to no one, I have made myself a slave to everyone, to win as many as possible. [20] To the Jews I became like a Jew, to win the Jews. To those under the law I became like one under the law (though I myself am not under the law), so as to win those under the law. [21] To those not having the law I became like one not having the law (though I am not free from God's law but am under Christ's law), so as to win those not having the law. [22] To the weak I became weak, to win the weak. I have become all things to all people so that by all possible means I might save some. [23] I do all this for the sake of the gospel, that I may share in its blessings.

We have called this team many names and the nick names never end. We may even call them "the 911 call team" of intercession. They could be called "the emergency response" team. They are the "hospitality team" of intercession. They can pray with anyone at anytime and flow with ease. They do not get unraveled with the mercy *or* the warfare intercessors, even when the two groups *may* be praying what sounds like "conflicting" prayers. In a very real sense the general intercessor is as much like Christ as any other intercessor. He was there for everyone and nothing was too hard for Him to deal with. He never stressed out over sickness disease, demons or death of people, Dutch Sheets tells the story in his book on *Intercessory Prayer*, about the young school boy who was drawing a picture and the teacher came and said to him, "Wow, that's an interesting picture you're drawing. What is it? The young boy said "why it's a picture of God." The teacher responded and said, "But nobody knows what God looks like" To which the young artists quickly smiled, saying as he returned to his drawing, "they will, when I get done".

Chapter 16 The Financial Intercessor: The Harvest Callers

Have you ever really thought about the fact that the very thought of the term "financial" intercessor, would pose a problem in the minds of a lot of people in the world? Think about it for a minute and the passage of Scripture immediately comes to mind about the love of money being the root of all evil. However, we are not talking about the love of money here. Instead, we are talking about the *provision* of money.

As we deal with financial intercession, we must understand that most everything in the world operates by money. As a matter of fact, when the Ecclesiastes writer made mention of the word money answering of all things, he probably had no idea what it would grown into. However, he did know how riches were effecting *his* life. Although I do not believe it answers *all* things, I believe it *is* an answer to most everything in our "*world*" system.

We may not see financial intercession clearly in scripture unless we read the bible with different "intercessory vision." There are several people who stand out as financial intercessors if you look closely. Let's look at a few considerations:

Abraham

Abraham may have been the first financial intercessor. When Lot went to a land that was flowing, because he thought he was choosing what looked like the best deal, Abraham went to a less prosperous *looking land.* Even though Abraham went to a land that did not look as prosperous his intercession before God was "glory" drawing. We see then as the man blessed by God walks into a land that did not look prosperous, it became prosperous because of his presence. Now that my friend, is true intercession. It may even be better titled a "prosperity" intercession anointing, because he didn't have to *ask* anything. It happened because of who he *was. He* was what the land needed. The land followed the man.

Jacob

Jacob could be labeled a financial intercessor as well. When he shows up to work on Laban's land, everything he does ends up prospering his father in law. He had the same Intercessory anointing on his life that his grandfather had. As we will see, it was in his genes. One of his sons carried the anointing into a strange country saving it and his own people with it.

Joseph

Joseph was a financial intercessor. He may be the most obvious and famous in all of scripture. It was his prayers, dream interpretation and hearing from God, that absolutely changed a generation in Egypt and save the lives of his family who was suffering lack. Joseph having been sold to into slavery, never stops using his gift of interpreting dreams. Wherever he goes, you see him finding favor and the favor of God finding him. He became the financial intercessor of a nation. If we could interview Pharaoh he would tell you that even though he didn't believe in Josephs God, he believed in his anointing. It even took a while for his own family to recognize, but *need* brought them to revelation.

Moses

Moses was a financial intercessor. We may see him as more of a "provisions" intercessor of sorts. Moses continued over and over to intercede for the needs of Israel as they were on their way to the Promised Land. His intercession for them made possible all of their provisions. Money is seen as capital that is traded for goods to meet certain needs. Moses did not just stand before God for food, but he stood before him to hear how to build the tabernacle. it was With God, in prayer, that we see Moses return asking those who are willing to bring exactly what was needed for the building.

Financial intercessors stand before God not just to get a download about money, but at times to hear specific strategies about where the money is to be spent, and how much is needed. Absolutely Moses has to be considered as a financial intercessor. Finances were seen much differently then. The trading of land, the trading of produce was predominant early and then the giving of money comes later.

Elijah

The uncommon financial intercessor we see in Scripture is the prophet Elijah. In First Kings chapter 18 he actually prays and says there will be no rain on the land until he gives word. That doesn't sound like financial intercession, but when he says that, he is talking about what the land will yield.

We were in worship service early one Sunday at a hotel (where we had started a new church). We were worshiping so, that it drew in a husband and wife. It was raining outside and I was urging the members to cry out "the harvest is coming." Traditionally, when it rains, people stay home on Sundays in an almost somber state as though it is a bad day. I received a revelation sometime back, that there is no harvest without rain, so that's what we were praising God about. The elderly Jewish woman asked could she say a word. I agreed to have her speak and she blessed us tremendously, confirming the revelation. She said that in the Jewish culture rain was a sign of God's blessing on the land. It would no longer be dry, bit would now produce, be fruitful. (I feel like praising God right NOW!)

So, when Elijah mentions no rain and then it will rain when he says so, he is talking about his intercession making the difference in their finances.. No rain, no crops! No crops, no finances! It's really that simple. Yielding of crops in the land was how every farmer made their living. You must agree, that Elijah was a financial intercessor.

Jesus

One scripture and you decide whether Jesus was a financial intercessor. The scripture where Jesus tells the disciple to go get the money out of the fishes mouth...

> [24] When they came to Capernaum, those who collected the two-drachma tax came to Peter and said, "Does your teacher not pay the two-drachma tax?" [25] He *said, "Yes." And when he came into the house, Jesus spoke to him first, saying, "What do you think, Simon? From whom do the kings of the earth collect customs or poll-tax, from their sons or from strangers?" [26] When Peter said, "From strangers," Jesus said to him, "Then the sons are exempt. [27] However, so that we do not offend them, go to the sea and throw in a hook, and take the first fish that comes up; and when you open its mouth, you will find a shekel. Take that and give it to them for you and Me." (Matthew 17:24-27)

The Challenge of the Call

In Wayne Gruden's book, *Politics According To The Bible,* he says this, "Sometimes people assume that Christians should not promote economic growth because that is materialism and materialism is evil, but I disagree. I do not believe that economic growth in itself is morally evil or simply the result of wrongful materialism. Nor do I believe that economic growth is something that is morally neutral. Rather, I believe that economic growth is in itself morally good, and morally good at what God intended."[96]

In March of 1930, President Hoover infamously declared that the economy would sort itself out, however the worst was still to come. We know that period in American history as "the Great Depression." The stock market crashed. People whose God was money, were committing suicide. Hotel managers were being quoted as saying that it got so bad that they were asking people were they renting a room to sleep in, or to jump from.

In recent years, (the 2000s), we have seen what we have labeled "a recession." The economy again has been challenged greatly. The job market has been scarce. People are fearful to say the least. The middle class has suffered, which is generally a sign that the poor have received "*new residents",* in their community. In other words, lower income and loss of employment has increased the poverty level and homelessness is a greater problem than ever.

> Grudem writes, "One of God's original purposes for human beings was to make the earth productive: Genesis 1:28 "And God blessed them, and God said unto them, Be fruitful, and multiply, and replenish the earth, and subdue it:

---

[96] Grudem, *Politics According To The Bible*, 269

and have dominion over the fish of the sea, and over the fowl of the air, and over every living thing that moveth upon the earth."

The word translated subdue is the Hebrew term KADASH meaning to subdue dominate bring into servitude or bondage...This expression in God's original command to Adam and Eve implies that he wanted them to investigate, understand, use and enjoy the resources of the earth. They were to do this as God's image bearers and with thanksgiving to God. This implies that developing and producing more and better goods from the earth is not simply a result of sin or greed or wrongful materialism, but something that God planned for human beings to do from the beginning. It is an essential part of how he created us to function." [97]

These are two contrasting scenes: the present reality that keeps surfacing (poverty/depression/recession) verses God's original intent. What gives? I mean, why are we continuing to live beneath our privileges, or our created worth? Is the problem with God? Okay, have you finished your laugh? Well now, we both must agree that it is certainly not!

"Houston, We Have a Problem"

On April 14, 1970, John Swigert Jr., James Lovell and Fred Haise Jr., were a part of the now famous Apollo 13 moon flight. The event has been made into a major motion picture starring Tom Hanks. There is a famous line in the movie that has been used numerous times since, to describe people's

---

[97] Ibid, 269

challenges: singer Whitney Houston's health and addiction prior to her death and even to describe stories about people being injured in over enthusiastic Wii (Nintendo game) play.

To set the record straight, the astronauts never said those exact words. They actually said, "Houston we "*had*" a problem. The keyword obviously there is "had." The problem they *had*, was not one that surfaced minutes before the call or as the call was being made. It was a problem that they had been watching and working on, but without success, and finally decided to alert headquarters that they needed some direction on what their options or possibilities might be.

Okay, so you should have an idea where I am headed. We have had a problem in the area of our economy for far too long. The current federal debt is over $17 trillion dollars. Two of the countries that hold the highest amount of our debt are Russia and China. Both of these countries have a history of dictatorship as opposed to democracy. Strangely, they were once known as bitter enemies of ours. The Bible says, in Proverbs 22:6 "The borrower is a slave to the lender." So now, does that that mean we are slaves to other "world power" countries that have governments which are diametrically opposed to our way of life? That my friend is tough to even consider.

The church, God's earthly body, instead of modeling financial/fiscal responsibility, has also been sucked into the cultural vacuum and finds itself in the same position as the government. Therefore, just as the United States, which has been perennially known as the richest country in the world, is now known as one of the biggest debtors, so too has the church come to be known.

Like these astronauts on Apollo 13, it's time to call headquarters and say the revised version, "Houston we have a problem

The Stimulus Package

When the economy was reaching its valley moments, President Obama and his team of experts put their collective wisdom together and came up with what we know as the "stimulus package". It was actually called, "the American Recovery and Reinstatement Act (ARRA) of 2009. Its idea was to immediately create jobs, provide temporary relief of those impacted most by the recession and finally to invest in things like health, education and energy.

One document said, "The rationale for our ARRA was from the Keynesian macroeconomic theory, which argues that during a recession the government should offset the decrease in private spending with an increase in public spending, in order to save jobs and stop further economic deterioration".

While I believe that we have the greatest institutions of higher learning in all of the world and the brightest minds come out of those institutions, they do not pale in comparison to the institution God gave to lead the earth. As a matter of fact all, the other institutions in America were established to aid the flourishing of this one. It is called the church, and it has the stimulus package already in its guidebook. Second Chronicles 7 verse 12 through 14 gives us why we are in our predicament in the first place and how we can get delivered from it.

> "Then the Lord appeared to Solomon at night and said to him, "I have heard your prayer and have chosen this place for Myself as a house of sacrifice. [13] If I shut up the heavens so that there is no rain, or if I command the locust to devour the land, or if I send pestilence among My people, [14] and My people who are called by My name humble themselves and pray and seek My face and turn from their wicked ways, then I will hear from heaven, will forgive their sin and will heal their land."

I know this sounds like such a simple plan and one that could be categorized by a team of political "experts", as ludicrous, however, the reason we are in the position we are in is because humankind has totally disregarded the will of God and gone after "it's own righteousness". The wisdom of men has us in this quandary. We always believe *we* have a better way than God. Therefore we adjust, restructure, and revise the word of God to fit our context, as if God did not foresee our generation and what it would be facing.

The government is in financial straits. The church is in financial trouble as well. Our cities are screaming with terror because people are out of work, and idleness *invites* iniquity. So now, what do we do? Let us get back to the Word. If MY people PRAY, I will HEAR and HEAL! It's that simple.

"And I Couldn't Hear Nobody Pray..."

J. W. Works published a song in 1940 with these words in it. It says, "... way down yonder by myself and I couldn't hear nobody pray. In the valley, ah couldn't hear nobody pray, with my burden...on my knees... trouble... A-couldn't hear nobody pray "

We are in DESPERATE need for intercessors to stand today. However, we just don't need *any* kind of intercessors, we need specialists. We need those who know where their passion is and purposefully pursue specific needs in the earth. That is why you are reading this chapter. We need your help to get out of this financial rut. This is especially the case for the kingdom crowd. We must follow the plan of God to line up with His will, so that we return to our position of authority in the earth. Financial intercessors must pray increase over God's people, but also discipline so that we steward it properly.

Ken Hubbard writes, "The world we live in runs on money. Money is the fuel that stokes the fires of commerce. Governments and businesses cannot survive without it. The nation's wealth is measured by its per capita income and its gross domestic product. It seems that more and more" haves" call the shots while the "have-nots" have little choice but to follow along. Everywhere, the "Golden Rule" applies: those with the gold make the rules."[98] If this is true, and it is, then why are we not praying a perpetual harvest into our coffers, stewarding our resources properly, so that we stay on the supply side and not the need side?

Breaking the Spirit of Poverty

One of the assignments of the financial intercessor is to be instrumental in breaking the spirit of generational poverty in our communities and churches. This is a serious issue. Most people who grow up in economically challenged conditions never get out of the mentality, even if they move from the physical environment. Poverty is a spirit! Take that to the bank!

The September 2012 Census revealed that one out of seven people in the USA are living in poverty. This is based upon income level, which we mentioned earlier, which places people in position to have "worldly" influence. However, when we put wealth into perspective and look at poverty in the spiritual realm, we come to an understanding that one purpose of wealth is for *blessing* others, not *bossing* them. We also come to an understanding that poverty is really: the curse of never having enough. No wonder my grandfather could declare that he was rich (not wealthy). Of course I considered him wealthy as opposed to rich, because of his wisdom. He never bought into the world's philosophy that we could be categorized strictly on income level. His riches were in his heart to give to many others, love and advise his family, providing for, and encouraging any and everyone no matter age

---

[98]Ken Hubbard and Nick Pagano, *The Morality of Money: Biblical Roads to Financial Freedom* (Hagerstown, MD: Fairmont Books, 2004), 27

creed or color to accomplish things they had potential to achieve despite cultural differences or challenges.

If true poverty is living in the state of never being satisfied, unable to stop dancing, then more people are in poverty then statistics could ever record or imagine. So we are dealing with two different, but very serious forms of poverty that help keep the world and the church divided. One is the lack of money with no clue on how to escape its clutches because of one's environment. The other, a lack of contentment, fueled by greed, that keeps yelling, "Show me the money," but never shares the wealth.

Financial intercessors must address both areas in prayer. Why? Because in a real sense, Pastor Ed Montgomery was right when he said, "poverty is nearly always connected with unrighteousness. It was the unrighteousness of an individual or the unrighteousness of the entire nation that brought oppression of pocket the people of Israel".[99]

Montgomery mentions several *poverty* influences that keep people in generational nightmares. I want to add to his list some practical things that people who struggle with financial issues need to be cooperating with in the natural, as we do our spiritual work.

> Credit card debt- it must be eliminated or put in perspective with what our income is.

> Overextended lifestyle- this is akin to credit card debt, but we cannot overemphasize this point. Many people are always trying to keep up with other people in their immediate surroundings, environment, neighborhoods, or place of employment. It is a competition thing that is very unhealthy.

---

[99] Ed Montgomery, *Breaking the Spirit of Poverty* (Lake Mary, FL: Destiny Image Publishers, 1988),

Trying to live out financial fantasies- "I always want to do this" "if I had enough money I would do this". "oh I will do it anyway".

Habitual borrowing, which we all know that the Bible says that the borrower is a slave to the lender. So, the question is, Even though we *say* we're not slaves we cannot quit our jobs until we pay off department stores etc.

Slothfulness with paying bills on time

Not having a budget-If you do not know what you're spending versus what you're making, you're probably in trouble

Eating out versus taking your lunch or preparing dinner at home is always more expensive.

A plan of escape- What is your one year plan. What is your five-year plan? Where do you see yourself 10 years from now? Do you see the place you desire to be? Have you begun to plan out how you're going to arrive at that place?

Financial intercessors are called to study statistics of the poor and the wealthy to discover their habits and work with the research intercessors, warfare intercessors and others to break this death spirit (curses: according to Deuteronomy 28).

The Purpose of Money: Covenant Contractors

I do not think most people ever really stop to think about the real purpose of money, why we have it, needed, or how to use it. As children of God, we should always know why we *have* money, why we *need* money, and why we *use* money. We are so busy acquiring money to: impress others; to feed our desires to be important; become more comfortable; or to improve our status so much, that we miss God will for us being stationed in specific places, around specific people. Come on friend! Here is the question, Are we here on earth to stay or are we on assignment? Really, we are what I call "Kingdom Covenant Contractors". We are sent into people's lives to help construct **covenant** in them *and* the world.

As a financial intercessor one of your assignments is to pray in Deuteronomy 8:18, which says, "But you shall remember the Lord your God, for it is He who is giving you power to make wealth, that He may confirm His covenant which He swore to your fathers, as it is this day" (NASB).

Therefore, we are not just praying in finances, we are praying in covenant wealth, so that we can build the kingdom of God. Everybody who comes to us claiming they need money, does not mean that we should be praying for them to receive money alone. They may be asking for it to establish the "opposing" kingdom. While we are never in favor of famine, we must agree with God that famine disciplines society and often makes many people more sensitive to the poor, because they now have at least tasted.

"The Wealth of the Wicked"

I am convinced that during recessions, famines, great depressions or times of scarce resources, that financial intercessors are in *greater* need for three reasons: First of all, people who do not normally give God their highest priority begin to turn to Him because their "green" God (money) is not working; Secondly, you very rarely have wealth transfer without a struggle; Thirdly, crises is the great equalizer and often causes people to see the needs of others in hopes that they do not end up becoming one of them. At times they may even feel that they can buy their way out, impressing God with a substantial monetary gift.

The wealth of the wicked is actually the result of fallen mankind (Genesis 3). Adam had it all in the garden of Eden. Eve sold her birthright for a moment of pleasure and Adam agreed with her. They signed over their rights to dominion, by submitting to a fallen, demoted, substandard creature's voice, over the voice of God.

When Jesus came, he came to restore our rights. *He* intercedes for the intercessors! I want to release something special to you. The wealth transfer has already been made. It has been deposited into our accounts. However, access to our accounts depends upon our revelation of righteousness (imputed: given to us because of Jesus). This is an area of which financial intercessors *must* stand in agreement in prayer. As a matter of fact, pray now for the wicked to get saved, then the transfer becomes a done deal.

Priests and Kings

Have you ever heard the philosophy that there are only two kinds of people in the church: priests and kings? In a nutshell, it says that all of us are there for a purpose. Most are there as priests. Priests get the day to day work done in the temple of God. They pray, minister to others, and basically intercede to God on behalf of others. They spend most of their time *inside* of the temple or in close proximity.

On the other hand, there is another group called "Kings". Their time is limited at the temple because of work schedule, but they do come faithfully to be instructed. However, their key assignment is to make money and invested into the kingdom work.

Jesus was approached by a rich the young ruler who wanted to know what he needed to do in order to attain eternal life. The first word to him had to do with the Word of God (the 10 Commandments), but the second, had to do with the will to do or to *be* the Word. He was admonished to help provide for, or make a difference in the lives of the less fortunate. He passed the first test, but failed the final. He was a "king" that did not use his anointing properly.

Jesus is walked as a "financial intercessor." He was calling in "the Kings" to walk in the anointing to assist where they are best able to do so. Now financial intercessor, you should be praying for every business owner to be sensitive to the needs of every community.

John MacArthur says, "Money in itself is neither righteous nor evil--it is morally neutral. However, money is an accurate measure of one's morality. When we refer to money we are referring to our medium of economic exchange, something so vital that it defines how we live from day today. In a cash-based society it might have been difficult to track one's use of money, but today a look over your check book ledger or credit card statement will easily reveal where your money goes. And where you spend your money determines where your heart is and what your life's priorities are (Matthew 6:20, 21). Someone who sees the pattern of your spending can fairly well discern the moral direction of your life."[100]

Blessed To Be A Blessing

I agree with the person who said that our talents, gifts and abilities are either used to attain wealth in a righteous way, or in essence we have stolen them from God, because we've used them to take more than our share of the pie. The purpose for every gift God gives us is to share it with *Him*, by way of sharing it with humanity.

Abraham the father of faith, is said to have been the wealthiest man on earth in his day. One Jewish internet source recorded this:

"The world knows of Abrahams Faith and his cattle, servants, sheep etc, but those in the Kingdom of Elohim also know of a specific

---

[100] John F. MacArthur and Jr, *Whose Money Is It Anyway?* (Nashville: Thomas Nelson, 2000), 4

calling and number that tells the "rest of the story". The number is "318". That's the number of trained (educated) men that Abraham personally "discipled," and what did Abraham train them in? The voice of YHWH, the charge of YHWH, the commandments of YHWH, the statutes of YHWH, and the laws of YHWH. The prime numbers between 7 and 49 add up to 318. The name Eliezer equals 318, Eliezer means: El is my help. Until YHWH revealed Torah through Moshe and then through haMashiyach, Abraham was the measure of a Man of YHWH. By YHWH's authority, the wealth of the wealthy is the property of the poor. YHWH makes people wealthy and He makes them poor. YHWH tests our souls to show us what is inside. Poverty sometimes visits the wealthiest of the wealthy, it is not only reserved for the poor or the poor. The wealthy man who wants, has much bigger "issues" than the poor who wants, the poor imagines wealth, the wealthy have it but remain impoverished by their wants".[101]

The financial intercessor prays privately and publicly for those who have been blessed to be a blessing as well as for those who challenge us to release our blessing on them.

Genesis 12:1-3 records the words about our father in the faith Abraham. The Bible says, "The Lord said to Abram, go forth from your country and from your relatives and from your father's house to the land which I will show you and I will make you a great nation and I will bless you and make your name great and so you shall be a blessing and I will bless those

---

[101] http://www.mashiyach.com/poverty.htm, Accessed July 21,2013

who bless you and the one who curses you I will curse and then you all the families of the upper shall be blessed"

My beloved are we not Abraham's seed? Well, should we not follow his footsteps? The same call is on our lives, Isn't it? He too was an intercessor, shouldn't we be?

Lin Johnson writes, "Your bank accounts have your name on them. Your paychecks are made out to you. You spend time, probably more than you want to, obsessing over your finances: whether you have enough money to pay your bills, if you can afford to buy what you want, if you can afford to retire someday. Even though you may review your money as yours, it's not."[102]

Financial intercessors have to have that revelation close to their heart every time they prepare to pray. You must be totally convinced that everything you have (that means you) belongs to God; you also must be convinced that you are stationed where you are to be praying for the church, that the church receive that kind of Revelation as well. The world will receive revelation based upon how the church images that revelation from God. We must change the philosophy that "life imitates art." We must be the initiators of a new philosophy that "life imitates the image of God," (which is His church). Get these following scriptures imbedded in your heart.

The year is the Lords, and all its fullness, the world and those who dwell therein. (Psalm 24:1 KJV)

For every beast of the force is mine and the catalog thousand heels. (Psalm 50:10 KJV)

I need is a good thing to receive wealth from God and the good health to enjoy it. To enjoy your work, this is indeed a gift from God. (Ecclesiastes 5:19 NLT)

---

[102] *Everything the Bible Says About Money* (Minneapolis, Minn.: Bethany House Publishers, 2011), 9

The silver is mine, and the gold is mine, see if the Lord of hosts. (Haggai 2:8 KJV)

For everything comes from God and exists by his power and is intended for his glory. All glory to him forever! Amen. (Romans 11:36)

As we near a close on this chapter on financial intercession, I want to leave you with four areas in which I believe every financial intercessor must be engaged, in order to effect the kingdom of light so that it makes a difference in the world:

    I. Partner Against Poverty
    II. Promote Harvest
    III. Properly Position the Saints
    IV. Prevent the Devourer

Partners Against Poverty

Throughout Scripture we are encouraged, provoked, admonished and even warned, to remember the poor. We have spoken to this end previously and will not dive fully, back into the same waters. However, it *is* worthy of re-emphasis. One cannot claim kinship with God then close their eyes to the needs of humanity. The early church was a shining example of coming together for fellowship *and* meeting needs of others. Note these three passages of scripture from the book of Acts:

Acts 2:44,45 says, "And all those who had believed were together, and have all things in common; and they began selling their property and possessions and were sharing them with all, as anyone might have need."

Acts 4:33-35 says, "And with great power the apostles were giving witness to the resurrection of the Lord Jesus and abundant grace was upon them all. For there was not a needy person among them, for all who were owners of land or houses would sell them and bring the proceeds of the sales, and leave them at the apostles feet; and they would be distributed to each, as any had need."

Finally, Acts chapter 11:27-30, Now at this time some prophets came down from Jerusalem to Antioch. One of them named Agabus stood up and began to indicate by the Spirit that there would certainly be a great famine all over the world. And this took place in the reign of Claudius. And in the proportion that any of the disciples had means, each of them determined to send a contribution for the relief of the brethren living in Judea. And this they did, sending it in charge of Barnabas and Saul to the elders."

The very heart of God is to see those who "*have*", partner with those who do *not* have. A couple of years ago, in the city where I am privileged to serve, a great gathering was called. It was a convocation of pastors from every denomination, culture and geographic area of our city. I was excited, to say the least, to attend his gathering. I desperately wanted to see what would take place. We sat for hours listening to presentations, looking at footage and statistics of how poverty effects crime, education and health.

I was sitting in the room, next to one of my colleagues and friend of another hue, who pastored in the suburbs of the city. He reached over and asked me a question. He said, with a tone of astonishment, "What is your take on all of this Darryl?" My answer was very direct. I said, "This is for you guys who pastor outside of the city. It is a sensitivity session. I see this every day. I live in this reality."

While I was there, I got a revelation about what we could do to address the sadness we were seeing. It seemed like such a God idea to gather all of these men and women from across the city who had a tremendous wealth of knowledge. I just kept thinking to myself, "Wow, every culture, every denomination, it must have taken a lot of work to get all of these people together." I knew many of them. I had sat in gatherings with them on other occasions, but never all of them from this diverse a background in one room, with the possibility of being on one accord. It was potential a Pentecost experience. This gathering had a wealth of resources as I said, however, what a waste if we did not actually *do* something with the information that we were receiving.

As I was sitting there, it hit me. Prepare something that we all could work on together. I began working on something immediately. I called it "MAPAP" (Metropolitan Area Pastors Against Poverty). I was ecstatic about the download I was getting from God about it. I assumed that the convener of the conference would be equally excited about a follow-up plan that would transform our city and be lead by "The Church".

I asked a simple question. What if the visionary pastors who lead wealthy churches partnered with visionary pastors who led inner city churches, and they combined their financial, physical, spiritual and intellectual resources, to take down poverty in the city? To make a long story short, I shared the vision and it was received with false interest and two years later, after two more empty convocations, we are still looking at the same old same issues.

Financial intercessors are called to pray for partnerships in our cities that will defeat poverty. This will take patience and endurance. As Job argues his case for his own righteousness, he says in chapter 31 verse 16 through 18 (MSG)

> "Have I ignored the needs of the poor, turned my back on the indigent, Taken care of my own needs and fed my own face while they languished? Wasn't my home always open to them? Weren't they always welcome at my table?"

As Job was pleading his case it is obvious that he lists three particular areas that man should never be guilty of neglecting if they are portraying a standard of righteousness:

the poor; the widow; and the orphan. He says, in essence, "I *am* guilty of being a sinner if I have failed in this basic area of love."

The one area I have noticed as a flaw in the church (universal), is our unenviable ability to overlook "Samaria". We are really good at internal fellowship, church work, family ministry and neighborhood evangelism to "our own kind". We even do well with foreign mission work, a place where we do not have to spend long periods of time touching people or building lasting relationships. However, we are very weak at reaching across town to people in our own cities who are unlike us socio-economically or culturally.

Promote Harvest

The financial intercessor has to be confident that God's *Word* is true. They must be undaunted in their faith. When Genesis 8:21 says, "As long as the earth remains there will be seedtime and harvest," they must be certain that they are not just praying in seeds (money) to be sown, but they are also praying in the proper harvest of those seeds.

The financial intercessor prays through the several stages that are required to get to the point of harvest. In that I am a city boy and have only been gardening for a few years, I am without question no expert. However, here are a few things I have learned from being a student of the process:

1) The ground needs to be tilled (sometimes more than once in a season)- The soil needs to be turned over, the grass and weeds up rooted so that new plant growth has unencumbered space to flourish.

2) Lime and other soil sweetening organic substance needs to be spread on the land

3) Seeds need to be planted at the right time. All seeds have a season where they grow best.

4) Plants need food- 10-10-10; Miracle Grow etc.

5) Patience- Knowledge of seed – knowing how long it takes seed to grow *down* (beneath the soil) before it grows up helps the planter not to become frustrated. Also, it helps you know whether the seed planted was washed away, did not get enough sun, a cold front killed it, some underground animal ate it.etc.,and it's not going to come up.

6) Periodic weed killing – protecting the plants future

7) God given element- sun and rain – we can produce things with our water and light, but they are not the same as natural nutrients from God's rain and sunlight.

8) Expectation- faith; preparation for harvest

Bad/Hard Ground

It is the job of the financial intercessor, as previously mentioned, to pray for the church as well as individuals who need money or resources, that they have the right covenant commitment. The impure heart that receives increase will cause crop failure for Gods earthly kingdom. Personal gain that does not advance the cause of Christ is in essence crop failure. It *is* harvest, but it actually is harvest that supplies another kingdom.

Financial intercessors pray for sweet spirits to surface. They pray for those who are totally given over to the fruit of the Spirit, walking in love and waiting for increase, so that they may impact the world in a greater way, with the fragrance of Christ

Right Timing

The financial intercessor must pray for funds to be placed as seeds, in the hands of those who need it, at the right time. The wrong time in the right hands, can cause poor judgment to take place (even for good people).

Seeds planted in the wrong season can cause crop failure as well. Every seed needs not only the right environment, but the right conditions. If you invest time planting watermelon seeds in the winter, even though it's an unusually warm week in the Midwest eventually the cold front will come and the seed won't yield increase. Likewise, you must know when to invest money. Therefore, the financial intercessor is always praying for their own personal wisdom, as well as for those who are *seeking* or *needing* their service/gifting.

Soil/Seed Food

The food for the seed is always in the richness of the soil. The seed gets its nourishment from the God-given soil. We are the soil. We need the proper nourishment in order to see our seed grow healthy/properly. Our food – miracle grow – is the Word of God.

Praying the Word is the life breath of EVERY intercessor. The financial intercessor must not just pray in money, but pray for its growth and for the soil to stay rich in God, uncontaminated by disease. Remember, the harvest is the seed that feeds the kingdom and eventually strengthens it to overtake the world.

Patience

The financial intercessor must exercise patience. Sometimes harvests are slow to manifest. Remember Galatians 6:7 and do not *get* discouraged or let the people you're praying *for* become discouraged either. Sometimes, there is no growth, because you do not have enough seeds in the ground. Do not forget, that our prayers and fasting are seeds, as well as our actions. That said, consider the possibility that many do not receive financial breakthroughs because *they* have not (or you the financial intercessor) planted enough seed in the ground (be it sowing into other ministries, praying in faith, fasting or making it happen for others by diligently working or serving them with our hands and tongues, to encourage them).

Remember Galatians 6:7,8 (MSG) which says, "Don't be misled: No one makes a fool of God. What a person plants, he will harvest. The person who plants selfishness, ignoring the needs of others—ignoring God!—harvests a crop of weeds. All he'll have to show for his life is weeds! But the one who plants in response to God, letting God's Spirit do the growth work in him, harvests a crop of real life, eternal life".

Weed Killing

Patience involves killing the weeds of doubt, discouragement, fear, and even people who are naysayers (of course I do not mean killing people literally). Do not be afraid! Be Like Jesus in Mark 5, put professional criers out of the room while you are interceding for a miracle. You cannot afford to allow any *weeds* around your plants. They suck off the nutrients and then choke out the life of the seed. Remember, the dominant seed takes the garden.

Again, we must use the spiritual pesticide of prayer, fasting and add things like positive confessions. When you confess the word, you kill weeds. They cannot grow in a fearless environment.

Expectation of Promises

Financial intercessors always expect God to do His job. Listen to a few passages of Scripture that promote the promise spoken from God's word:

Matthew 7:7-9 "Ask and it will be given to you; seek and you will find; knock and the door will be opened to you. For everyone who asks receives; the one who seeks finds; and to the one who knocks, the door will be opened."Which of you, if your son asks for bread, will give him a stone? Or if he asks for a fish, will give him a snake? If you, then, though you are evil, know how to give good gifts to your children, how much more will your Father in heaven give good gifts to those who ask him!

John 14: 13,14 Whatever you ask in My name, that will I do, so that the Father may be glorified in the Son. If you ask Me anything in My name, I will do it.

Luke 6:38 Give, and it will be given to you. They will [a]pour into your lap a good measure—pressed down, shaken together, and running over. For by your standard of measure it will be measured to you in return."

2 Corinthians 9:6-8:- WHOEVER SOWS GENEROUSLY WILL ALSO REAP GENEROUSLY *God is able to make all grace abound to you *So that in all things *At all times *Having all that you need * You will abound in every good work

2 Corinthians 9:9:- HE HAS SCATTERED ABROAD HIS GIFTS TO THE POOR *Now he who supplies seed to the sower and bread for food *Will also supply and increase your store of seed * And will enlarge the harvest of your righteousness * You will be made rich in every way * So that you can be generous on every occasion

MALACHI 3:10 :- BRING THE WHOLE TITHE INTO THE STORE HOUSE *See if I will not throw open the floodgates of heaven * And pour out so much blessing that you will not have room enough for it * I will prevent pests from devouring your crops * And the vines in your fields will not cast their fruit

PSALM 112:5 :- GOOD WILL COME TO HIM WHO IS GENEROUS AND LENDS FREELY * Surely he will never be shaken * A righteous man will be remembered for ever * He will have no fear of bad news * His heart is steadfast, trusting in the Lord * His heart is secure * He will have no fear * In the end he will look in triumph on his foes * He has scattered abroad his gifts to the poor * His righteousness endures forever * His horn will be lifted high in honour

Finally the financial intercessors assignment is this:

Prevent The Devourer

The financial intercessor is a teacher of others, as well as one who talks to God. They at times, are called to counsel those for whom they are interceding. There is no need to pray in a harvest that is going to eaten up by the enemy.

Many people write requests to my wife and I to pray for debt cancellation, or increase on the job, raises, new jobs, financial breakthroughs. My very first thought, as I am praying, is usually a question. "Are they a tither?" They are claiming to sow for a harvest, but with stolen seed. You cannot steal seed and expect ***His*** harvest.

Tithing is the bill we owe for the seeds we sow. Only money beyond the tithes can be designated as the seed for harvest, thereby having expectation of God's favor on it.

There are several passages of Scripture I want to leave with you as a financial intercessor, as you press forward to accomplish the assignment God is giving you. Again, know that you are more than one who stands in the gap between heaven and earth merely to talk to *God* alone. You must speak to *humans* regarding their obedience as well. Let's begin with Malachi chapter 3 verse 6 through 12 in the NLT:

> [6] "I am the Lord, and I do not change. That is why you descendants of Jacob are not already destroyed. 7 Ever since the days of your ancestors, you have scorned my decrees and failed to obey them. Now return to me, and I will return to you," says the Lord of Heaven's Armies. But you ask, 'How can we return when we have never gone away?' [8] "Should people cheat God? Yet you have cheated me!
>
> "But you ask, 'What do you mean? When did we ever cheat you?'"You have cheated me of the tithes and offerings due to me. [9] You are under a curse, for your whole nation has been cheating me. [10] Bring all the tithes into the storehouse so there will be enough food in my Temple. If you do," says the Lord of Heaven's Armies, "I will open the windows of

heaven for you. I will pour out a blessing so great you won't have enough room to take it in! Try it! Put me to the test! ¹¹ Your crops will be abundant, for I will guard them from insects and disease.[a] Your grapes will not fall from the vine before they are ripe," says the Lord of Heaven's Armies. ¹² "Then all nations will call you blessed, for your land will be such a delight," says the Lord of Heaven's Armies.

Now beloved, Compare verse 10 and 11, to the following Amplified version which says:

¹⁰ Bring all the tithes (the whole tenth of your income) into the storehouse, that there may be food in My house, and prove Me now by it, says the Lord of hosts, if I will not open the windows of heaven for you and pour you out a blessing, that there shall not be room enough to receive it.
¹¹ And I will rebuke the devourer [insects and plagues] for your sakes and he shall not destroy the fruits of your ground, neither shall your vine drop its fruit before the time in the field, says the Lord of hosts.

Notice the words "*your income*" in verse 10 and *devourer* in verse 11 which are followed by... "And he shall not destroy..."

I do not know about you, but I find that interesting. It does not say "*they*" will not destroy, meaning insects and plagues. It says "*he*" which suggests that there is some *being* behind the destruction of our harvest. *Satan* is that being. He is the devourer that fights the harvest God has for us. John 10:10 says it plainly, "The thief comes only to steal and kill and destroy; I came that they may have life, and have it abundantly".

Note again, that **God** will "*prevent the devour*", the enemy himself, from eating the crop. God does that when the individual who comes to us asking for financial breakthrough or open heavens, is actually obedient to His Word. His Word says for us to bring the tithe and the offerings to the storehouse. If a person has not been obedient to the word and will of God, then for us to pray for a harvest or financial increase, despite their disobedience, we are in actuality praying *against* the Will and Word of God.

James 4:2 says we do not have certain things because we have not asked God for it. But it concludes in verse 3 with the statement that sometimes we do not receive because we ask wrongly. That means we are asking for things that are for our own glory or outside of the will of God.

Financial intercessor, you can never do that!

Here are some other scriptures you must meditate on if you are serious about this area of intercession. If you truly want to know what you are praying for and why, as well as help other people with questions getting answers to why their prayers are or are not being answered the way they desire, then study before you intercede.

Genesis 4 Abel offers God a sacrifice (offering)

Genesis 8 Noah offers God a sacrifice (offering)

Genesis 13:18 Abram, of his own free will, offers a thanks offering

Genesis 14:17-20 The first mention of tithe is here and it was *pre-law*

Genesis 28:18-20 Jacob tithes as thanks for safety on his journey to find a wife

Exodus 25:1, 2 Willing is the watchword for giving

Exodus 35
Exodus 36:1-7 The people had a heart to give generously beyond the tithe

Leviticus 27:30-34 The tithe is holy; not doing it has a penalty like a retuned check fee

Numbers 18:25-30 Teaches how Israel was to use the tithe

Proverbs 3:5-10 Trust is the foundation for giving...period

A Few New Testament references to tithing and giving in general:

Matthew 23:23
Luke 18:9-14
II Corinthians 8:1-5
II Corinthians 9:6,7
Hebrew 7:4-9

A final note: tithing is not the end all. It is the foundation. The Christ follower is seeking to give....ALL.

May your prayers shake the windows until the body of Christ is fully supplied for every purpose and assignment our Father calls us to. Please Do Not forget me...as you pray.

Bibliography

Alves, Elizabeth *Becoming a Prayer Warrior: a Guide to Effective and Powerful Prayer*. Revised ed. Ventura, CA: Regal, 2003.

Alves, Elizabeth (Beth), and Barbara (Tommi) Femrite & Karen Kaufman. *Intercessors*. Ventura, Calif.: Regal, 2000.

Arthur, Kay. *Lord, Is It Warfare? Teach Me to Stand: a Devotional Study On Spiritual Victory*. 1st WaterBrook Press ed. Colorado Springs, Colo.: WaterBrook Press, 2000.

Eastman, Dick. *Intercessory Worship: Combining Worship and Prayer to Touch the Heart of God*. Ventura, Calif: Regal, 2012

Elwell, Walter. Evangelical Dictionary of Theology (2nd ed.). Grand Rapids: Baker Book House, 2001.

Elmore, John Hull & Tim. *Pivotal Praying: Connecting with God in Times of Great Need*. Nashville: Thomas Nelson, 2002.

Engle, Lou with Catherine Paine. *Digging the Wells of Revival: Reclaiming Your Historic Inheritance through Prophetic Intercession*. Shippensburg, PA: Destiny Image Publishers, 1998.

Evans, Tony. *Kingdom Man: Every Man's Destiny, Every Woman's Dream.* Tyndale House. Carol Stream, IL 2012,

Frangipane, Francis. *The House of the Lord: God's Plan to Liberate Your City from Darkness.* Lake Mary, Fla.: Charisma House, 1996.

Goll, James W. *Prayer Storm: the Hour That Changes the World.* Shippensburg, PA: Destiny Image, 2008.

_____ *The Lost Art of Practicing His Presence*, Shippensburg, PA: Destiny Image, 2005

_____ *The Seer* by Shippensburg, PA: Destiny Image, 2004

Grudem, Wayne. *Politics According to the Bible: a Comprehensive Resource for Understanding Modern Political Issues in Light of Scripture.* Grand Rapids, Mich.: Zondervan, 2010.

Goudeaux. Phillip. *Finances God's Way,* Sacramento, CA: Calvary Christian Center G Publications, unknown

Hewing, Pernell. *Calling Forth The Bride of Christ For Intercession,* Whitewater, WI. Sanctuary Word Press. 1995.

Hughey, Rhonda. *Desperate for His Presence: God's Design to Transform Your Life and Your City.* Minneapolis, Minn.: Bethany House Publishers, 2004.

Hubbard, Ken, and Nick Pagano. *The Morality of Money: Biblical Roads to Financial Freedom.* Hagerstown, MD: Fairmont Books, 2004.

Husband, Darryl F., *The Altared Life,* Lulu.Com, LIFE More Publishing, Richmond, VA. 2008

_____ *Living a Lifestyle of Fasting* Lulu.Com, LIFE More Publishing, Richmond, VA. 2011

_____ *I Am the Church and My Name Is House of Prayer.* Lulu.Com, LIFE More Publishing, Richmond, VA., 2011.

Johnson, Lin (compiler) *Everything the Bible Says About Money.* Minneapolis, Minn.: Bethany House Publishers, 2011.

Kimbro, Dennis. *What Makes the Great Great.* Reprint ed. New York: Broadway Books, 1998.

Machiavelli, Niccolo. *The Prince.* Boston: Bedford/St. Martin's, 2005

Maher, Bridget, Editor. *The Family Portrait: A Compilation of Data, Research and Public Opinion On The Family.* Washington, DC: The Family Research Council. 2004

Merriam-Webster Online Dictionary Merriam-Webster, Incorporated, 2005

MacArthur, John F., and Jr. *Whose Money Is It Anyway?* Nashville: Thomas Nelson, 2000.

McMurry, Douglas. *Richmond Awakening.* Richmond, VA: Bethlehem Books, 2005

_____, And The Transformation Richmond Team. Richmond, VA: Bethlehem Books, 2003

Montgomery, Ed. *Breaking the Spirit of Poverty.* Lake Mary, FL: Destiny Image Publishers, 1988.

The New Century Dictionary, Appleton Century Company, New York, NY, 1948

NIV Naves Topical Bible, Zondervan Publishing House, Grand Rapids MI, 1994

Otis, George, Jr. *Informed Intercession.* Ventura, Calif.: Renew, 1999.

Prince, Derek. *Promise of Provision, The: Living and Giving from God's Abundant Supply.* Bloomington, Minn.: Chosen Books, 2011.
_____. *Secrets of a Prayer Warrior*, Chosen Books, Grand Rapids, Michigan, 2009

_____. *Shaping History through Prayer and Fasting.* New Kensington, PA: Whitaker House, 2002.

Sheets, Dutch. *Intercessory Prayer: How God Can Use Your Prayers to Move Heaven and Earth.* Ventura, Calif: Regal, 2008.

_____ *The Beginner's Guide to Intercessory Prayer.* Ventura, Calif: Regal, 2008.

Strong, James, *New Strong's Exhaustive Concordance of the Bible*, Nashville, TN: Thomas Nelson Publishers, 1990

Trueblood, Elton, Patricia Trueblood. *The Recovery Of Family Life.* New York, NY: Harper & Brothers. 1953

Vine's Complete Expository Dictionary of Old and New Testament Words. Thomas Nelson, Inc., Nashville, TN, 1984, 1996

Wagner, C. Peter *Territorial Spirits: Practical Strategies for How to Crush the Enemy through Spiritual Warfare.* Shippenburg, PA: Destiny Image, 2012.

_____ *Warfare Prayer (Prayer Warrior).* Revised edition ed. Ventura, Calif: Regal Books, 1997.

Warren, Rick. *The Purpose-Driven Life: What On Earth Am I Here For?* Grand Rapids, Mich.: Zondervan Publishers, 2002.

Wattles, Wallace D. *The Science of Getting Rich: Attracting Financial Success through Creative Thought.* Rochester, VT: Destiny Books, 2007.

Webster's II New Riverside Dictionary Revised Edition, Boston, MA: Houghton Mifflin Company, 1996

Wiens, Gary *Bridal Intercession: Authority in Prayer through Intimacy with Jesus.* Oasis House, Grandview, MO: 2001,

Wilhite, Jud. *Pursued: God's Divine Obsession with You.* New York: FaithWords, 2013.

Zondervan. *Comparative Study Bible, Revised.* Revised ed. Grand Rapids, MI: Zondervan, 1999.

www.mashiyach.com/poverty.htm, Accessed July 21,2013

About The Author

Bishop Darryl F. Husband, Sr., is the Senior Pastor of Mount Olivet Church in Richmond, Virginia, and founder of Life More Abundant Ministries. He is also the founder and Presiding Prelate of the Alliance of Ministries Equipping Nations (A.M.E.N.) – a fellowship of churches and men and women of God with the anointing in their lives to break strong holds and release the area troops to continue the work they begun.

For more than 30 years he has served as Senior Pastor to the Mount Olivet Church, a multi-cultural congregation in the inner-city community of Church Hill in Richmond, Virginia. Since becoming the pastor, Bishop Husband has founded and implemented many ministries, including L.I.F.E Church West and the soon-to-be announced L.I.F.E Church South. His passion for training leaders is evident through the growing Mount Olivet Leadership Education Network (MOLTEN) Bible Institute and newly formed Church Leadership Training School.

Bishop Husband received his Bachelor of Arts Degree from Illinois State University with a major in foreign languages. He later matriculated at Virginia Union University where he earned his Master's Degree in Divinity at the Samuel D. Proctor School of Theology. He earned a Doctor of Ministry degree in 2004 from Virginia University of Lynchburg. He has also done doctoral studies at Boston University.

Bishop Husband has several spiritual connections. He and Co-Pastor Sherrine Husband are connected and covered by Bishop Wellington Boone's Fellowship of International

Churches. Bishop Husband also serves the Full Gospel B C F International as the Southern-Atlantic Regional Director for the International Intercessory Prayer Ministry under Bishop William Murphy Jr. Bishop Paul S. Morton is Presiding Bishop.

Bishop Husband has a heart for people of different ethnic backgrounds and has traveled to many countries around the world doing leadership workshops and leading worship: Scotland (Aberdeen, Glasgow), England (Colchester, Preston, Manchester, and London), India (Chennai, Nagaland, Mumbai), Brazil, Finland, Cuba, Ukraine, and Africa (Liberia, Ghana, Benin, Cote d'Ivoire, and Cameroon) and Israel.

He is the author of *The Altared Life, Discovering The Winner Within; Daily Readings From Proverbs-For Building Character, Living A Lifestyle Of Fasting: Breaking Through To The Best You, I Am The Church and My Name is House of Prayer, Your Body: The Temple of God, Dad- The Missing Link: Healing The Wounds Of A Generation* and *Transitioning the Traditional Church*, his doctoral work. Also pending is a life motivational book entitled, *Success Is the Plan God Has for You*. Bishop Husband released his debut CD *Instrument of Praise* in 2006 and in 2007 released his CD *I Was Made to Worship,* and currently working on his third project.

Bishop Husband is married to the former Sherrine Charity. They are the proud parents of Darryl Frederick Husband II, Gabriella Sherrine Agape Husband, Jason Oliver and two others the Lord gave, Daytriel McQuinn and Eric Elam.

Other Books by Bishop Darryl F. Husband, Sr.

The Altared Life

Discovering the Winner Within :Daily Readings from Proverbs for Building Character

Living a Lifestyle of Fasting: Breaking Through to the Best You

I Am the Church and My Name is House of Prayer

Your Body: The Temple of God- The House Where His Presence Lives

Dad, The Missing Link: Healing The Wounds Of A Generation

Books may be purchased online:
http://www.lulu.com/spotlight/darrylfhusband